Fishing for
Love on the Net

Fishing for Love on the Net

A Guide to Those Searching for Love

MYLES REED, JR.

iUniverse, Inc.
New York Lincoln Shanghai

Fishing for Love on the Net
A Guide to Those Searching for Love

iUniverse books may be ordered through booksellers or by contacting:

iUniverse
2021 Pine Lake Road, Suite 100
Lincoln, NE 68512
www.iuniverse.com
1-800-Authors (1-800-288-4677)

Because of the dynamic nature of the Internet, any Web addresses
or links contained in this book may have changed
since publication and may no longer be valid.

ISBN: 978-0-595-42491-7 (pbk)
ISBN: 978-0-595-90310-8 (cloth)
ISBN: 978-0-595-86824-7 (ebk)

Printed in the United States of America

Cover graphic artist—Marco Rodriguez: www.rodboards.com

Author photo by Michelle Piccolo Hill of Piccolo Photo: www.photopiccolo.com

I dedicate this book to Bodil and Philip, the loves of my life.

Special Thanks

I want to first thank God through Jesus Christ for such an amazing gift in this book. I also want to thank William Reed and Andy Andow for encouraging me early on when the book was just a thought.

Special Thanks

Content

Introduction

Today Internet dating seems almost commonplace. You would think that everyone was doing it, given the vast amounts of money spent on advertising and the number of Internet matchmaking sites. The heavy hitters in the industry have produced numerous commercials. Almost every time I watch television after work, I see a really well done advertising spot for eHarmony. The couples seem very happy and genuine about the mates that they found through this service.

Additionally, there is Match.com and its TV and radio spots. All of these commercial messages are full of excitement and energy not only for love but also for how the Internet can play a primary role in bringing some joy to one's life. For many people, the idea of Internet dating is new, so there is an awakening to the possibilities. For others, these ads inject hope that the Internet experience, which had previously conjured up feelings of suspicion, might be something worth considering.

What these ads present are the finished products: people happy with the outcome and satisfied with the decisions to take a leap into this burgeoning space. The cake is baked. It is not clear, however, how the cake got baked. What was the recipe?

Many people have tried online dating with no success. The steps necessary to secure love online still remain a mystery. Many more people are sitting on the sidelines, waiting and wondering if they should try it. Online dating is a phenomenal avenue to meet that special someone. I am going to share with you six years of experience that will take the mystery out of online dating. I will show you that there is a process that is unique to online dating and is inescapable. The truths of my experience will give hope and clarity to those serious about finding love.

My Desire for You

My desire is that you become emboldened to take the first step into online dating. If you have already dabbled with online dating, I want to motivate you to feel energized once again about the potential for finding love on the Net. For everyone else, I am presenting to you a glimpse into the community of millions around the world who are looking to make a connection online.

I was one of online dating's early adopters, circa 1999. This was back when you were really considered weird for engaging in this kind of experimentation. I learned a lot about this new tool, this new social movement. I learned a lot about myself. I certainly learned a lot about other people. It was an odyssey that lasted more than six years. I was taken through several profound and intriguing encounters.

We like the happily-ever-after sentiments presented in the media about online dating: it feels good; it leaves you hopeful. There is, however, an underbelly to the experience of meeting people online. As with anything, there are ins and outs as well as ups and downs. What I want to do is reveal a bit of that to people the world over. The Internet makes the world a very small place. Surprisingly and fortunately, the factors that drive Internet dating are strikingly common across many continents. I want to give people a sense of what it is really like to take a ride out into the ocean of the Internet and go fishing for love.

This is what I give to you: the benefit of things that I've learned from the errors that I've made, as well as the encouragement I've received from the things that went really well. I have always been told that feedback is a gift. I want to give you this gift: my feedback on myself so that you will be wiser and closer to having the relationship that you desire.

Chapter 1

Why Are We Here?

The Internet is incredible. It is surely one of the top five life changing inventions of the twentieth century. Its potential is still evolving before our eyes. The Internet can be a bit intimidating. It is big. It can seem like a door into nothingness, into space, yet it is full of all kinds of things. It is quite the juxtaposition—grandness and seeming emptiness serving as the conduit for individuality and intimacy.

When I started writing this book some time ago, I wasn't sure how this topic would resonate with readers. Online dating was once something that no one would consider doing; the prevailing opinion was that something was wrong with you if you engaged in online dating. Now advertisements for online dating can be found on the Internet and on TV. Today the online dating phenomenon has caught the attention of everyday people, as well as at least one celebrity. It has been rumored that celebrity personality Joan Rivers has even dared to try to find love on the Net.[1] Even with this increased visibility, many people are still unsure if Internet dating really works. Does it lead to great relationships? The answer is yes; it does work. I'll show you why and how.

It Is All about Love

Why would someone even consider using the Internet to establish a relationship? The answer is *love*—four letters, one syllable. It is about romantic love—not the love that you have for your grandma, your girlfriends (ladies), or your buddies (guys). It's the kind of emotion that can cause you to act a little crazy at times.

We are willing to do a lot to find love. We pursue it like fiends. Love can compel behavior that, when glanced at in the rearview mirror of life, can cause us to either wince at the pain that we somehow endured or smile at the blissful moments. It doesn't always end in tragedy. Many happily ever afters are created in the pursuit of love.

In the process of chasing down love, often somebody will get hurt, even when it works out well. In spite of the many perils, love is a wonderful thing, which is why we will never stop pursuing it. In fact, we often go to extreme and experimental lengths to get it. Yes, even a box full of transistors and memory chips—the PC—and the Internet will not be ignored if they can deliver real love or the prospects of it.

Let's Give People the Full Story

The ads on television about online dating suggest that it is as easy as one, two, three. All the commercials say that you just have to fill out a profile or a questionnaire and, like magic, you'll find your life mate. You will soon be ready to provide your own testimonial. Like effective movie previews, these are great teasers. What none of these clever commercials do is describe what Internet dating is really like. Sure, you have to fill out a profile or a questionnaire, and after some time and effort, it is possible that you will find a life mate; however, the online dating experience is much more complex than this.

Because there is so much more to online dating than what is presented on the commercials, I am left wondering, where's the rest of the story? Do the "previews" of online dating do a sufficient job to enable you to be successful? No, they don't. People are given a sandwich with no meat. They show you the beginning and the end. As the old lady from the commercials in the 1980s cried, "Where's the beef!"

The entire melodrama that is inextricably linked to finding love is missing. What is behind the bright smiles and hugs of the people that you see on TV? What will you have to confront to obtain what the commercials promise? *Fishing for Love on the Net* gives you that story. That is why you should read this book.

Where Do People Traditionally Find Love Today?

Bars

Oh yes, the bars have always been a main option for people in search of potential mates. This practice is a bit counterintuitive: people looking for that special someone among a group of slightly inebriated souls. Sure, everyone that you talk to will tell you that a bar is usually not the ideal place to meet your next husband or wife. Contrary to all the sage advice, these places stay packed. Sometimes this pearl of wisdom is even expressed by someone as he or she tries to stammer through a conversation at 1:30 AM after at least two too many drinks. This is usually not a good place to begin a life together or at least a period of dating bliss. There are, of course, always exceptions.

Work

We spend most of our time there. It is hard to resist. People are looking their best, and you are around them eight to twelve hours a day. Why wouldn't you consider this a prime place to find love? It is a common place, but it is filled with potential professional and personal landmines. I don't even want to recount for you my personal experiences that reinforce this point. I had three near misses with "real" love at work, but it was not to be. Again, there are exceptions.

Where You Worship

There is church, the synagogue, or wherever you choose to worship. These are good places, right? However, you know how dating can go. You are generally unsuccessful until you get married. Dating is a continuous stream of relationships that are destined to end until you find the right person. They start and then last for a while, but usually they come to an end. There is no need to create drama and broken hearts in your place of worship. One too many of these occurrences can make the holy day less restful and comforting than you expected. I usually treaded lightly there.

Hobbies or Activities

There are many activities that require interaction with people where the possibility for coffee and possibly dinner exists. There are classes (art, language, and others where there are people to interact with). Are you light on your feet or looking to meet someone light on his or her feet? Salsa is always good. I have always loved salsa. It has that built-in icebreaker. I'm serious. Think about how awkward the initial interactions between two people can be. With salsa, you have to touch—it is hand to hand or hand to shoulder, but there is touching. This is huge. Okay, that's my plug for salsa. Like other options, hobbies can be hit-and-miss.

Your Friend's Referral

There is also the blind date. It could be that guy your best friend thought would be great for you, or it could be that woman your buddy's wife just knew would be your type. People sometimes see you differently than you see yourself. After the date doesn't go so well, you are left to wonder about your friends, "Do they really know who I am?" I'm not criticizing referrals; many lasting relationships have budded from these introductions. The other benefit is that usually the person has been vetted to a degree, so you can feel relatively comfortable that the "crazy factor" has been reduced.

You know the "crazy factor": You've met somebody, and he or she seems great. He had nice shoes. She had great hair. Then, two months into the relationship, the "crazy factor" begins to rear its ugly little head. Fortunately, it is very easy to identify. The person just starts acting unusual, a little crazy. Perhaps he or she shows up unexpectedly at your job all the time. Such behavior might seem sweet at first. Then it gets scary. Expressions such as "I really missed you. Where have you been?" are warning signs, particularly when it is 9:55 AM and you didn't get off the phone with him the previous night until 2 AM. You can't avoid people like this. The risk of encountering the "crazy factor" is possible no matter where you meet someone. This is true even on the Internet. It is just an occupational hazard of dating.

People Are Considering Cyberspace

Today, people are not doing away with the traditional methods of meeting people. They are simply expanding the list of the potential places to find love. Humans are always looking for new areas to conquer. The settlers of this country kept pushing westward in search of new territory until they hit the Pacific Ocean. We weren't content just being on this planet, so we went to the moon. Now, the Internet is the next frontier in dating. Dating on the Internet is a relatively new cultural phenomenon, but it has really found its identity over the past several years. Not too long ago, if you were finding dates on the Internet, you were supporting a new "crazy factor." Oh, I know from personal experience.

I recall defending people who would take a chance to find love in such a way. In reality, I was defending myself to them. I was exploring a new frontier. I felt kind of cool because I had discovered this new pond of potential mates to fish in. Quite frankly, it felt like my "dirty secret." In 1999, all of my acquaintances were publicly bashing this new thing called "online dating," while I was at home trying to figure out this thing. I felt that I had to be, as Elmer Fudd would say, "vewy, vewy quiet" or risk social ostracism.

I had to maintain a duality. By day, I was a "normal" dater, cruising the bars and clubs with buddies, taking salsa lessons, and maintaining a keen eye at work for the next dame that would be mine. All the while, I was racking up some noticeable weekly hours peering into this nascent space of the Internet. I was looking to see who was looking along with me. You don't have to be so concerned today. The current has changed.

Online Dating Is Here and Is Not Going Away

My, my, how things have changed. Online dating is now a full-fledged niche with publicly recognized company names that have become the symbols of love on the Internet—names like Match.com, MySpace. com, and eHarmony. More important, people—and I mean millions of people—have "mainstreamed" this channel. This space is as viable an option for love as your local bar, your friend's blind date recommendation, or any new rapport begun at the job. It is amazing when you consider the progress this online industry has made in just over five years.

Only a few pure Internet business models have managed to become mainstreamed and thrive: search portals like Google, Yahoo, and MSN; low-cost travel; and online retail sites, led by the two pillars of Internet commerce, Amazon and eBay. Several years ago, news segments couldn't have discussed the Internet without at least briefly mentioning the most popular and profitable online business, adult entertainment. Online dating has proven to have similar staying power.

Are You the Only Person Considering Online Dating?

No, you are not alone; many people engage in this activity. First, take a look at the number of people with computers. In the United States alone, there are over 61 million households with a PC. Approximately 90 percent of these households have Internet access.

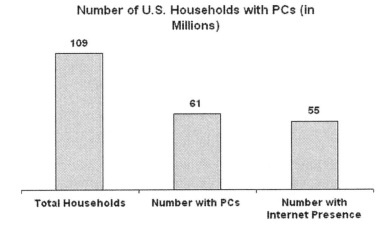

Number of U.S. Households with PCs (in Millions)

Source: U.S. Census Survey, September 2001[2]

This number is not trivial, and we can be certain that this number has grown rapidly from 2001 to 2007. In fact, "The advertising intelligence service from Nielsen Monitor plus said that while total media spend for such efforts was $149 million in the U.S. in 2004, it rose to $310 million the following year, and hit $430 million from January to November of 2006."[3] This isn't just a U.S. phenomenon. CNN.com also reported a boom in online dating across western Europe. It is clear that Internet dating has taken root. This is good news for you, because there will be more people for you to consider dating.

The adoption of online dating should continue because of the "viral marketing" that is happening around people's successes and failures. I frequently hear people talk about their own or their friends' experiences with online dating. These stories will continue to seed feelings of familiarity and curiosity. I ask those early adopters who tried and were not successful and may have given up to reconsider online dating. If you are new to this realm, don't be afraid; instead, be excited that Internet dating will give you an opportunity to improve your dating fortunes. I offer you my hand as we walk through my experiences. You will learn something.

Internet dating is real, and it is available to you.

Celebrity Endorsement of Online Dating

Dr. Phil, the country's leading talk show host on relationships, has partnered with Match.com. I think that this says two things: (1) the potential to find someone online exists, and (2) relationships are still complex and a little advice should always be welcomed. I will give you solid guidance on how to use online dating services so that you can find someone that you feel is worth your while. In the process, by following my suggestions, you will put yourself in a good starting position to build a solid relationship.

Making a promising Internet connection is an essential step toward happiness, but relationships require effort to make them thrive. This is most likely why the folks at Match.com thought that Dr. Phil would enhance the experience. I can respect what Dr. Phil and Match.com are attempting to do with his affiliation, but that is not what I'm primarily trying to do.

My primary objective is to help you find someone, leveraging this tool and my expertise. You can't benefit from relationship advice without first having a relationship. Remember, no matter where you have met people up to now, this is about love and how the Internet can help you achieve that.

It may seem a bit unlikely, but to me there are many similarities between the process of finding love and going fishing. It is all about having the right equipment, finding the right fishing hole, and using attractive enough bait, which will hopefully result in a great catch. The following pages will elaborate on how online dating can be exciting and will improve your chances to find some success while fishing for love on the Net.

This Book Is for Every Single Person

Adoption Segments: Single People Considering Online Dating

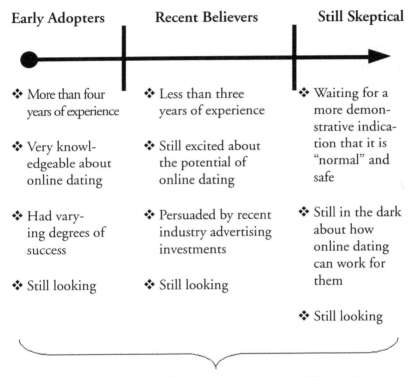

Early Adopters	Recent Believers	Still Skeptical
❖ More than four years of experience	❖ Less than three years of experience	❖ Waiting for a more demonstrative indication that it is "normal" and safe
❖ Very knowledgeable about online dating	❖ Still excited about the potential of online dating	
❖ Had varying degrees of success	❖ Persuaded by recent industry advertising investments	❖ Still in the dark about how online dating can work for them
❖ Still looking	❖ Still looking	
		❖ Still looking

Fishing for Love on the Net has something to offer each group

What This Book Is Not

People should not look to this book as a way to correct problems that you are having with someone that you met online. This is about how to find someone new online. There also won't be guidance on how to nurture a relationship. Relationships are complicated and require a lot of effort.

Ladies, you will not see a reference to the man's inherent need for respect, ego stroking, and support from his woman. Men, you will not see within these pages how a man must demonstrate his love for his woman in a way that is important and recognizable for her so that she knows that she is truly loved. I won't be talking about the need for communication and quality time with your partner or how important it is for couples to be intimate. I'm going to leave that to Dr. Phil and those in his trade.

I will show you how to use Internet dating effectively to find someone for romance.

A Recap Before We Pull Up Anchor

- We are online because of our *compelling desire for love.*

- Advertisements on TV give the *beginning and the end* of the Internet experience—where's the beef?

- This book *gives the middle that is necessary* to reach the end.

- Traditional ways of meeting people have not become ineffective, but online dating has earned a *legitimate place on the list.*

- The *mainstreaming* of online dating is evidenced by celebrity affiliations and the millions of global participants.

Chapter 2

Why Online Dating Will Work for You—The Conditions Are Right

Trust me when I say that you will not benefit from a simple twelve-step list on how to most effectively use the Internet to find a mate. There are so many twelve-step methods to accomplish practically everything. We have become accustomed to them and a bit limited by this approach. Please resist that inclination. Creating relationships requires thoughtful consideration. Remember, I am talking about people—individuals like yourself who have depth and personality. Online dating requires a balance of active steps and an appreciation for the context in which they apply.

People live their lives within a context. You can't learn a foreign language properly without understanding the culture of the country in which the language is spoken. The combination of technical grammar with cultural dynamics brings clarity and a sense of authenticity to the effort. Likewise, you cannot understand how to use online dating to create social networks and relationships without understanding a bit about technique and the context in which this tool exists to build sufficient confidence to stay the course. I will give you sufficient techniques, but context setting is important.

How does a society get to a place where something as personal as the process of creating a relationship full of emotion can be transformed and transacted in an almost arm's-length manner? The answer is that the same foundational elements that make the Internet so universally embraced make finding love on the Internet possible. Look at our lives. PCs are everywhere, and Internet use is widespread. Here are some elements that make Internet dating work.

The Great American Drift—We Are Less Social Now Than We Were Thirty Years Ago

Families Don't Eat Together as Much as They Used To

If someone had invented the Internet and Internet dating in one evening in his or her basement and introduced it to the world for commercial use in the 1970s, it would have flopped instantly. The American social structure was more communal then. Families ate dinner together more often. After dinner, many families watched television together. Families bonded when they ate together and laughed together. Face-to-face contact was essential.

Today, families don't eat together nearly as often. Many single people live outside their parents' home and more than likely in another town. There is less "face time" with the family, yet relationships continue to grow. All of this has enabled people to feel comfortable in relationships even when there is less actual time together, as one might experience with online dating.

Nobody Wants to Go Outside and Play Anymore

Years ago, teenagers played with each other outside for hours, until it was too dark to play. What was central for children was that they were physically together. They would have enjoyed a range of things: board games, tackle football, basketball, baseball, roller-skating, and so on. All of these are examples of collective socializing that helped create adults who were more likely to be involved personally and physically in social encounters. The dominant way of socializing and entertaining oneself was oriented around groups, but this has materially changed.

If video killed the radio star, as the song suggests, then video games killed children's group play. This change began in the late 1980s with the introduction of Atari and Pong. This led to Nintendo and Donkey Kong. Now we live in an age of the seemingly unending battle between PlayStation and Xbox. Each incredible advance in graphics and imagination has drawn our children closer and closer to the television and the game box and further away from group play. Video games have helped to increase the satisfaction that people derive from sitting in front of a box of electronics.

With families eating together a little less often and children playing together a lot less often, America has slightly drifted away from itself. We are resilient. We have adjusted. We have learned to thrive, in spite of it all. Because our socializing dynamics have changed, your chances of success with online dating have improved dramatically.

We Have Learned to Thrive on Communication That Doesn't Require Our Physical Presence

We Have a Love-Hate Relationship with E-mail

The change in social dynamics can be seen even in the workplace. Before the 1990s, the only way to give a message to someone was to speak in person, handwrite a quick note, speak on the phone directly (there was no such thing as voice mail), or type a memorandum. Today, it is all about e-mail. E-mails are everywhere, especially for the average American worker. Every day workers have to face the constant waves of red e-mails (meaning unread e-mails) that cross the shores of their in-boxes. A term like *crackberry* didn't exist in the 1970s. Someone who obsessively checks his or her e-mail on a Blackberry can be said to be checking the crackberry for new emails. E-mails hound us, but we seem to like the pursuit.

You Have Been Fired!—Check Your E-mail In-box

In the workplace, so much important information is given over e-mail. Things like company earnings, the announcement of a colleague's new promotion, or bonus details are all being communicated via e-mail. One company decided to push the limits of how we use e-mail. In 2006, in the United States, RadioShack informed four hundred of its employees via e-mail that they were going to lose their jobs.[1] How would you feel after receiving an e-mail like this after wolfing down a bagel and some Starbucks coffee? After adjusting to the shock of such a communication, you might think, "Oh, no they *didn't!*"

It is difficult enough to be let go from a job, but getting fired is infinitely more biting when you receive the news in this manner. Once the story broke, most people thought that the decision was heartless and executed with poor judgment. Sure, there was united disdain for how this was handled, but it certainly is quite telling about how we think e-mail can be used. Although RadioShack used the online medium to sever relationships, with online dating, the conditions are right for you to have the opportunity to create a relationship.

Living in the Wake of the Changes

Some might say that it is sad that our society has changed and has possibly become colder. The reality is that the great "American drift" and our evolution in methods of communication have left us with new attitudes about people and how we communicate. All of this makes Internet dating possible and offers you a chance for success.

The Same Rules Required in Developing a Relationship Still Apply

Don't think that dating online has somehow changed the way relationships work. Let me give you an example of this. I saw an episode of *Divorce Court* one afternoon. A wife and a husband were filing for divorce. They had met online and married shortly after meeting in person. They were filing for divorce because the wife felt that her husband was a mama's boy. He was equally fed up with her because she treated him like a child. These two spouses were going at each other furiously. The mother of the husband was barking at the wife about how much she hated her. It went downhill from there.

From looking at these two, one might conclude that it is completely unadvisable to look online for a spouse or even a girlfriend or boyfriend. Our society has changed, and our ways of communicating have as well, but certain things have remained the same. No matter where you meet someone, whether online, at a bar, at school, at work, on vacation, or anywhere, you can't avoid the effort necessary to determine whether this person is the right one with whom to build a relationship. Meeting people online is a great new thing, but there is nothing new about how relationships work. Don't forget that.

A Recap Before We Pull Up Anchor

- The conditions are *right* for online dating to work for you.

- American has *drifted from itself* a bit.

- E-mail communication has become a *strange bedfellow*.

- We are very *comfortable communicating* important information by e-mail.

Chapter 3

Benefits of Online Dating

I spent six years meeting people online. There were times when the benefits of online dating were clear. I was making great connections and enjoying myself. There were other times, however, when I was in slumps and felt a little discouraged. If you are already sold on Internet dating, you should still review this list. It will reaffirm why you are putting effort into online dating. If you participate in online dating long enough, you may go through your own slump and need a reminder about why online dating is great and why it has benefits. For the people who are new to online dating, this chapter should energize you even more.

Online Dating Companies Offer a Service That Meets Your Needs

Most companies that are trying to sell you something, whether a product or a service, they are attempting to satisfy the four Ps of marketing. If they can do this, the result will usually be a happy customer who has

19

purchased the specific good or service. The space of online dating and the majority of companies that offer this service have done this well.

The Four Ps of Marketing are Sufficiently Satisfied, to Provide the Service You Need			
Product	**Price***	**Place**	**Promotion**
Virtual socializing communities Millions of people -You -Everyone else online	Relatively low -Sometimes free -Generally $20–$30 per month	Service provided wherever you desire -Your home -Your office -Anywhere there is Wi-Fi connection	Companies consistently invests in ads -Frequent television commercials -Celebrity endorsements -Internet ads

* You can usually take advantage of discounted pricing when you purchase several months of the service at once.

Online Dating Is Available to People at Differing Stages in Life

The obvious segment of people who might find the Internet a good place to make connections is single people who have never been married. The good thing is that online dating is not for just the "never married" group. Unfortunately, at least 50 percent of U.S. marriages fail.[1] Because most people don't desire a life of unending solitude, they will, at some point, want to get back out there. They will want to establish a relationship with someone. Divorced people can also go fishing for love just like the other "never married" single people.

The same applies for the widowed. It may be difficult to get back out there after the tragedy of losing a spouse, but there is always someone looking for a partner, and that person just might be looking for you.

No matter what stage you are in life, Internet dating is available to you.

There Are No Special Restrictions on Who Gets Access

Popular nightclubs often use special criteria to determine who gets in and who doesn't, such as inclusion on a guest list, special attire, and so forth.

On the Internet, there are no special qualifications needed other than payment of a membership fee. Your name doesn't have to be on a guest list. You don't have to dress a certain way or have a certain amount of charisma. You can enter an online dating site and be as active as you would like, or you can figuratively hold up the wall—whatever is your pleasure.

All you need is a profile. Remember that this access is more than local: it is national and even international. Meeting people on the Internet will give you complete and equal reach. You can hang out with people from wherever you desire. Other than the New York subway system, not many places create an environment where everyone is on a level playing field. The $2 fee will take the millionaire uptown to the same site that it will take the college freshmen without a job; it is an equalizer. Dating online is also the great equalizer.

You Are Free to Dictate the Ways You Want to Experience the Sites

You can flip through profiles and people-watch until your eyes begin to burn from staring at your PC monitor. If you so chose, you could quit your job, sit in your pajamas for ten days straight without taking a shower, and people-watch, and no one would order you to take a shower. No one would ask you to stop searching. There is not a two-drink minimum. There is no bouncer, unless if you do something nefarious like hack into the Web site's database. Then you might get a knock on your door from your local police. There are no closing hours, no last call for alcohol. No one will be bothered by your presence. It is all up to you.

Gives You the Chance to Survey the Person Before Making Contact

People have a nosy bone. It is similar to a funny bone, but instead of being funny, it is all about looking into some situation or somebody's life in progress. Usually, the situation has nothing to do with you. We get a small amount of naughty pleasure by being a silent participant in someone else's life. We watch or listen to them without them knowing that we are there, following every little detail.

Why do you think that the television show *Big Brother* is successful around the globe? People love watching people's lives unfold before them. We just love watching "real" people break up and make up, get angry and be nice, and act deceitfully and extend a gesture of kindness. They reveal it all for us to see on *Big Brother*. It is popular in the United States, and similar shows have popped up around the world.

By looking at the myriad of profiles, you gain a better idea of what someone is looking for in a mate. You find out what people think of themselves. You also find out what motivates the person you think looks so great in his photo on the beach in the Caribbean. You can't glean this relevant data from just a pretty face that you see across a crowded room. We get to gather all this information without so much as a salutation. There is no need for a sheepish "Hi … how are you?" until you are sure that you want to make that confident greeting. Meeting people online is perfectly suited for the voyeur in all of us.

Requires Less Time

We are time-strapped. Everybody is looking for balance. We are overworked and don't have as much time as past generations. This doesn't apply only to married couples with two children. There are plenty of single people struggling to find more time to do the things that they want. We are always looking for ways to do things faster in order to save time.

This need for efficiency is everywhere. It is part of our society. The Internet takes an insane amount of data, distills it into the information that you requested, and delivers it to you within seconds. Now how convenient and time-saving is that? It would take you a very long time to introduce yourself and find out personal information about ten people in any given day. With the Internet, vast amounts of high-quality information can be provided in a matter of seconds.

Convenient—You Determine the Time

When do you want to explore the online dating sites? Do you want to do it before you go to bed on Friday night after rewatching an old episode of *Law & Order* with Lenny Briscoe? Or would you prefer to do it just before you go to bed on Tuesday after working twelve hours? Maybe you'd rather do it before you have lunch on Saturday or before you head out to work on Monday morning. You can experience the benefits whenever you want. There's no happy hour to plan around. You can do this from the comfort of your own home, morning, noon, or night. It is on your time.

No Age Limit

The notion of making a connection with someone online, whether for friendship or for something more significant and intimate, is not just available for the millennials (those now in high school and college). It is also for Gen Yers (people in their twenties), Gen Xers (men and women roughly in their thirties and early forties), and baby boomers (those in their midforties to late fifties). In fact, because so many people are living very active lives well after retirement age, seniors are using the Internet to meet companions as well. Just recently, it was reported that seniors in their sixties and seventies are venturing online as they socialize in their retirement communities.[2] As you can see, your age doesn't matter. It is just a number. Online dating is truly for everyone, which means that you can find a person of any age.

More Options

We have become a nation of people who cannot make decisions without at least five alternatives before us. We need to have options. Ask yourself, how many channels do you have on your cable or satellite service: 200? 300? You have even more options when you add in pay-per-view. How many travel Web sites do you research before you buy an airline ticket? Even people who traditionally loathe the idea of window-shopping will check two or three travel sites before they book. It is so easy that it's almost negligent to not check.

The Internet provides an unprecedented number of choices. In a way, it is a shopper's paradise—it presents a near endless list of options. Online dating, at the click of your mouse, gives you a tremendous set of options. A prospective male companion can be from Seattle or Florida. A prospective female partner can be a country girl from Tennessee or an easygoing Midwestern girl. I don't suspect that you will get bored very quickly.

These dynamics make it possible for an enormous number of people to fish in this space. With so many people online, just about anyone can find a suitable partner. Therein lies the big benefit: online dating will increase the number of people that you can potentially meet and thus increase your chances of finding a mate. This phenomenon has changed the lives of millions of people, and they are not going back to the way things were.

A Recap Before We Pull Up Anchor

- Online dating offers *a lot of benefits*.

- The service provided *meets your needs* to help you find a mate.

- It is suitable for people at *different stages* in life.

- There are *no restrictions* on who can access the sites.

- You *dictate the terms* of how you access—you can have it your way.

- You can *survey the person before* you make contact.

- It *requires less time* to find a potential mate.

- It is *convenient*.

- There is *no age limit* to restrict who can access sites.

- There are *more options* from which to choose.

Chapter 4

How to Think about Online Dating Sites

Where do you start if you want to find love online? Which sites should you visit? You'll see quickly that this space is big and that there are plenty of people for you. First, turn on that PC. You can, of course, do this whenever you want. Remember, it is convenient. Forget the Internet dating sites for now. Go to any search engine site, such as Google.com, Yahoo.com, or MSN.com.

Type in something as simple as the word *dating*, and you should get a hefty list of items to scour. Here's what I got when I tried.

Google	49.5 million results
Yahoo	378 million results
MSN	118 million results

Of course, no one has time to sift through this many results. So let's try another word.

When I tried the word *relationships*, I got the following results:

Google	92 million results
Yahoo	197 million results

MSN   28.1 million results

When I tried the word *love*, I got the following results:
Google   150 million results
Yahoo   1.3 billion results
MSN   270 million results

I hit the mother lode with the word *love*.

As you can see, there are tons of paths to pursue. You can waste a lot of time exploring all the results or even a percentage of them. You may want to try a number of routes, so it is best to organize your efforts.

How to Categorize the Portal Where You Might Fish for Love

Here's how to think about the sites that are explicitly set up as portals for dating. I have found that there are three types of sites:

- **Mainline dating sites**—Their primary business objective is to be a central meeting place or market for people who want to find others or who want others to find them.

- **Multipurpose sites that offer online dating**—These do a substantial number of things in addition to being dating portals, such as providing news or selling something.

- **Specialty dating sites**—Their objective is similar to mainline dating sites; however, they cater to particular sectors of the population, such as Christians or people who live in a particular city.

Here's a small set of them.

Mainline	Multipurpose	Specialty
Match.com eHarmony.com Perfectmatch. com Dating.com Lavalife.com True.com uDate.com MySpace.com	Personals.yahoo. com Craigslist.com MSN.com Google.com	Jdate.com Jlove.com American Singles. com Interracialsingles. net Blacksinglescon nection.com Christiancafe.com City-specific sites

Pick the Site That Is Right for You

I have used all three types of sites. The kinds of people that I found on the mainline sites and the multipurpose sites were very similar. These sites usually capture the broadest range of personality types, and are frequented by people of diverse backgrounds. Just about every type of personality (outgoing, creative, introverted, etc.) can be found on these two categories of sites. Both of these also have substantially more members to choose from than the specialty sites. Last, both mainline and multipurpose sites have the largest international populations. In short, these two categories give you the broadest spectrum of people and the largest number of people.

Sometimes people identify must-have criteria when they search for mates. Specialty sites can be a great way to facilitate that objective. Keep in mind that most specialty sites have a much smaller member base than the mainline and multipurpose sites, but you can more easily target the criteria that are most important for you. Because of the tighter-knit communities, I did notice a higher level of camaraderie from the people that were on the specialty sites.

Of course, everybody using a dating site is looking for a mate, so there is camaraderie over this point. However, it was not only my impression but others disclosed as well that people felt even more in sync on specialty sites because they shared the same special interest. They seemed to have a higher level of excitement about the site because they were one significant criterion closer to finding a mate who was best for them. It felt a bit like a club than the other types of sites because member participation was centered on this common interest or identity.

All three types of dating sites were valuable to me. You'll find that some people belong to multiple communities—they fish in multiple ponds simultaneously. I always found it funny when the same woman would appear in two separate searches on two separate sites. There are multiple ponds of people in which to place your rod and reel. When fishing for love, some people are putting in a little extra work to increase their chances. I recommend considering all three types, but picking the site or combination of sites that offers the best fit for you.

Will There Be Enough People from Which to Pick?

Here are some general statistics of one major mainline site from a set of queries that I conducted. Because I was a single man in America, my eyes were set on finding a woman who lived somewhere on this planet. The question that I had was whether there would be enough women for me to select from. My first query was pretty straightforward. The criteria allowed me to cast a wide net.

Men seeking women—Never married
25–50 years of age
No other criteria indicated

Search Results: Actual Number of Women

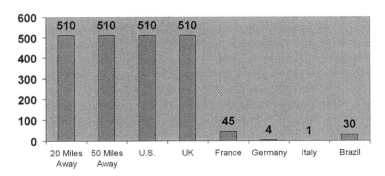

So, I have over two thousand women from which to select. You can try people that are local or far away. Well, if you are in the United States or the UK, you have plenty of options. If you live in the United States and are looking for someone in another country, there are far fewer people available to you on this particular mainline site.

I was wondering whether women have the same number of options to consider. I entered this query, and this is what I got:

Women seeking men—Never married
25–50 years of age
No other criteria indicated

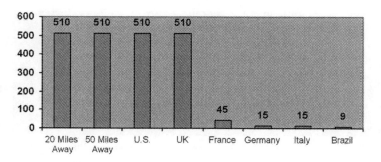

Search Results: Actual Number of Men

I found that women have access to the same number of potential mates. So you start with around two thousand people. If you decide to flip through only 1 percent of these people, you'll still have about twenty profiles to read.

We all know that the divorce rate has increased over the previous twenty years. There must be large numbers of divorced people still looking for someone special.

How Are Divorced People Embracing Online Dating?

Men seeking Women—Divorced
25–50 years of age
No other criteria indicated

Search Results: Actual Number of Divorced Women

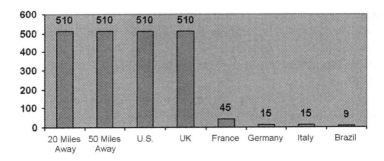

As you can see, even those who are divorced have a large number of people to select from. I suspect I would get the same result if I conducted a search from a woman's perspective, because a divorce produces both an available woman and an available man.

It's as Though Your Face Is in the Paper

Online dating is both private and public. Posting your profile on the Internet is like printing your profile in the local paper, but the profile will appear in many cities across the country. I am always amazed by the scope of the Internet. You can make what seems very distant—someone who lives on the other side of the country, for instance—seem very local, quite effortlessly. Sure, you may receive a message from someone in your hometown, maybe even someone who lives right down the street. However, it is also highly probable that the message will be from someone on the other side of your state and possibly the other side of the country. You may live in West New York, New Jersey, but you may receive a message from someone who lives in Seattle, Washington.

Don't think that this is just a U.S. phenomenon. You will make contact with people from around the globe. It is like going abroad without having your passport stamped. You might live in Sicily, Italy, and get a message from a person in Milan, Italy. It goes even further. You may live in Detroit, Michigan, but guess what? This person who sent you a message could be from Berlin, Germany, or vice versa. What do you do with that? As you know, sometimes it can be difficult to get to know someone from your hometown. Now, you could be presented with the possibility of getting to know someone from another country and culture.

All of this is good news for you. Your pool of potential mates is made substantially larger because of this, and thus your chances for success increase as well.

A Recap Before We Pull Up Anchor

- There are *lots of information* about love and relationships online.

- Mainline, multipurpose, and specialty sites can *meet a variety of needs*.

- There are *plenty of people* for you to consider, whether you are male, female, never married, divorced, or widowed.

Chapter 5

My First Experience

Looking for the Big Catch after a Long Voyage at Sea

Alaskan crab fishing is one of the most dangerous professions in North America. These courageous men and women endure harsh weather conditions and rugged work on a ship that will be tossed to and fro so that they can bring back a large booty of delicious crustaceans. As dangerous as the job is, it has been described as a once-in-a-lifetime experience; however, it is suited for only uniquely brave souls.

In a way, dating is similar. Setting your sights on love can be one of life's most dangerous pursuits as well. We joke about how many tears have been shed. We reflect on the wounded hearts that needed long-term mending in order to make pursuing a relationship meaningful again. Oh, if this were just a one-time folly, we could all shrug off the pain caused by these occurrences. However, despite the perils, we go back out on the high seas of life in search for the supposed "large booty" or the big payoff: the love of our life.

I have been one of those courageous fishermen. You are probably wondering whether surfing the Internet for love worked for me, the six-year veteran. The answer is yes. Now I will share with you some of my experiences, which will show you how it worked for me.

My First Internet Date—The Maiden Voyage

Ah yes, my first Internet date. Yeah, I can remember her face, but I can't quite recall her name. That was an interesting time for me.

The year was 1999. I was about a year out of a serious relationship. I had proposed to a woman about a year and a half prior; she had said yes but later got cold feet. My little heart was broken. I guess I was in shutdown mode; I was trying to repair my wounded emotions, which had been bruised when I was tossed on the shores of Heartbreak Island. I remember my friends having sympathy on me because I looked so pitiful.

I was like many single people at that time. I was living life the best way that I knew how. I was living alone in Manhattan in a one-bedroom apartment. I was pretty committed to my job. I was logging long hours. I have always been an early riser, so I would get up at 4:30 AM, hit the gym, arrive at my desk between 7:30 and 8 AM, and put in about ten to twelve hours. That was my routine, Monday through Friday. After about a year, I really started to get that itch to get out there again.

My hectic life left me with insufficient time to do many of the things that people do when they look for a mate. I didn't have much time for clubs or happy hours. I didn't have much confidence in those kinds of gatherings anyway. I got curious about Internet dating and thought that I would try it out. I knew that it was a new thing, so I decided that I would keep it to myself. I didn't expect it to take up too much time, so it fit in perfectly. I figured that at least I could experiment from my home without going out unnecessarily. I didn't even tell my close friends initially. As supportive as they usually were, they shared most people's opinion of online dating—"People who look for other people online are a little weird."

Those Nights of Solitude

When I started with online dating, I didn't expect the nights to provide such solitude. If there had been a camera filming me back then, maybe the setting in my apartment would have looked a little weird. It would be a Friday night. I was usually exhausted from the week, so I usually didn't feel like going out late. I needed to recuperate. I had my PC and desk jammed into the corner of my small bedroom. There was hardly any room to walk between my bed and my desk. The PC was practically in my bed. It was a typical New York one-bedroom, a bit undersized. I would be online at around 10:30 or 11 PM. All the lights would be out except the desk lamp, which shone directly onto my PC screen and the keyboard. Miles Davis would play in the background, and I would explore the Net for a few hours or until I got tired. That was my process: Friday nights, the PC, the lamp, and Miles Davis.

Because the portal that provides access to online dating is usually in your home, in most cases there won't be other people around. More than likely, it will be just you, your PC, and the tapping of your fingers on the keyboard. However, with all the Wi-Fi hot spots in coffee bars and airports, you can search wherever you feel comfortable.

Finally, a Catch

When I first created my profile, I was very hesitant to put my picture on the site. I'll talk to you about what to consider when creating a profile shortly. I didn't want to be outed, so to speak, as a closet Internet dater, so I tried to be incognito. I eventually got a woman to respond to my picture-less profile. We had good conversations for a few days. She was living and working in Manhattan, so I thought, "Great. Let's meet."

She was like me, an early adopter. She had a profile without a photo. She was equally hesitant about the world—or possibly our coworkers, family, and friends—thinking that she was so pathetic that she needed to rely on this new, potentially unsafe, and obscure way to find a date. At least that is what we both thought they would think.

I was a novice with no picture, and yet I was still able to get a response. This was very encouraging for me. The other person had to take a risk in making contact with me. She knew less about me than I am sure she would have liked. People are sometimes willing to take a risk, and that should be encouraging for you.

How Long Should You Wait Before You Meet Someone?

When should you meet someone in person? Should you wait a certain number of days? Should you wait until you've acquired a certain number of contacts? It all depends. There is a correlation between how long you've known the new person and the quality of your communication that impact the risks and the potential for success.

Risky	Most Ideal	
• The person is still very much a stranger—physical safety concern. • The higher lever of engagement generates some comfort.	• The person has shown consistent engagement. • The amount of meaningful information that has been exchanged creates comfort. • Increased chance of success.	High-Quality Dialogue
Most Risky	**Risky**	
• The other person is very much a stranger—physical safety concern. • The other person may not be very interested in you—potential waste of time.	• The person has been around but is still not familiar enough for you to know if a face-to-face meeting is worth your time.	Low-Quality Dialogue
Less than seven days	**More than seven days**	

If you are in regular contact with someone for more than seven days and the quality of your dialogue is good, you have an increased potential for a good first meeting.

She Was Nice Enough to Date Again

I had certainly been talking with this fine young lady for more than seven days, and the conversation quality was pretty good. We met in midtown for dinner on a Saturday evening. Midtown was a good choice for her, because there would always be a lot of people around. This was important for her safety, just in case I turned out to be a maniac. Ladies, for your first meeting, as a safety precaution, I highly recommend open areas that have a lot of people. Don't go by a guy's house on your first date just because he said that he wanted to cook you dinner. He might be dreamy, but it is too risky.

We had a pretty good time during dinner. I also recall being relatively pleased that her physical appearance wasn't terribly different from what I had imagined. To top it off, her personality was generally pleasant. In spite of what people might whisper about people who date online, she wasn't a strange person, desperate for any sort of attention. She was just as normal as I thought I was. All in all, that dinner passed the test for me to ask her out again. After the meal, we went to Central Park to chat a bit in order to walk off the dinner.

It was getting late, so it was time to catch a cab home. We shared a cab. Attempting to be a gentleman, I offered to have it take her home first. As we rode, we continued our light but enjoyable conversation. We reached her apartment and decided to kiss each other to close out the evening. This is how most people hope to conclude their first dates.

Good-bye and Thank You, Ms. Okra, with Gracious Appreciation

We were in the front on her apartment, ready to end what was a really solid first date. We started out with a standard peck that led to a more involved kiss. This was great, or so I thought. Much to my significant disappointment, she was the most horrible kisser that I had ever encountered. While our lips were locked, I was screaming in my head, "Oh no! This can't be happening! This is totally gross!" It was like kissing a bucket of okra. My grandmother used to make okra for my grandfather during lunch. I thought that it was slimy and gross then, and my opinion of okra hadn't changed. It was the messiest and gooiest kiss I had ever shared up to that point, and it remains the worst kiss I've ever experienced. I knew that there was no way to get over the "gross out" factor.

After I figuratively wiped my face, we said good night. We exchanged courteous smiles, and the evening was done. On that bumpy ride home to my apartment in that New York City cab, I had mixed feelings. On the one hand, I felt as though I needed to brush my teeth and gargle with the strongest mouthwash money could buy after doing the tonsil cha-cha with a bucket of okra; on the other hand, I was really grateful to that woman for taking a chance on me. She helped me gain some confidence in Internet dating. This experience was the start of an odyssey that would last over six years.

Of course, I was never going to see her again. Well, that is the nature of dating, isn't it? Someone might be a nice person initially, and then, after spending a bit more time together, you realize that maybe you are not the best match for each other. This will be the case for you too, so don't be bummed about it what it happens. Even though the evening ended in a tragic exchange of bodily fluids, there was some solace for me. She was my first. They say that people never forget their first of anything. I won't forget her either. Thank you, Ms. Okra.

A Recap Before We Pull Up Anchor

- Searching for *love can be potentially emotionally dangerous*, with the prospect of a great reward.

- Communicating with someone new for more than *seven days with high-quality dialogue* is the best indication of when it is a good time to meet.

- It is common to meet someone who initially *seems right* but later turns out not to be.

Chapter 6

Getting Started

Okay, if you want to be serious about this, you have to get your profile up and loaded with a picture. I have talked to a number of people who are curious about how to get started, and I tell them to put up a profile with a picture. It's that simple. They tell me, "No way. I don't want people knowing that I am online. I would be embarrassed. They might think that I am desperate." Thank God for common sense. I quickly reply that if they are noticing you online, guess what? They are looking too and are just as "desperate."

You have to be fully committed. An American television drama series used a great analogy to demonstrate commitment. When you have a plate of ham and eggs for breakfast, not everyone is equally committed to the meal. The pig is really committed, whereas the chicken isn't so committed. The pig has to literally give itself in order to make the ham possible. It is a one-shot deal for the pig. It is not so serious for the chicken. It can lay eggs for breakfast today and for many more meals to come. Life goes on for the chicken.

You won't have to physically give yourself to be successful online, but you want your commitment to be more like that of the pig than that of the chicken. It starts with having a good profile.

The Profile

Your profile is effectively a sales statement about you, what you offer, and what you require. Don't feel pressure to have the perfect profile in order to woo potential mates; your profile doesn't have to be Pulitzer Prize material. It should at least contain basic information: where you are from, some physical description of yourself, and a small paragraph about who you are and what you are looking for. I prefer profiles that reveal a bit of the person's personality, something that is a bit more distinctive.

You Have to Take Some Risks

You have to take a risk and reveal a part of who you are. You always want to be honest and true to yourself. God has made everyone unique, so sharing a bit of that uniqueness is an excellent way to enable your profile to stand apart. After meeting new people, we tend to remember their distinctive hobbies, passions, or philosophies. Such information generates interest. Perhaps you like to study Italian in your spare time and dream of owning a summer villa in Florence, or perhaps you love animals and find yourself walking into pet stores to window-shop for your next dog or cat. It has to be something that is authentic to you.

Avoid Being Loquacious—Shoot for Being Substantive but Not Overbearing

Your profile doesn't have to be a thesis. If your description of the kind of person you desire is five paragraphs long, you have overdone it. You'll have a difficult time finding a man or a woman who can meet half of your requirements. You will also drive people away by intimidating them. The same holds true for your description of yourself. A five-paragraph description is too long. Save some of that information for an e-mail exchange or a conversation on the phone. Whenever I encountered profiles that were way too long, I would abandon my review partway through. I just didn't have the patience. Other people don't have the patience either. No one wants to wade through the

War and Peace version of your self-description. Just share some details about yourself so that the other person can have a solid understanding of who you are.

Photos Are a Must—Everyone Is Photogenic, at Least to Some Degree

Photos are an essential component of an effective profile. You must have a photo if you are really going to be serious! Remember the pig. I made my first Internet connection in 1999 when many people were hesitant about online dating, so not having a photo with your profile was much more acceptable back then. Today, people are much more comfortable with online dating and expect to see a face.

Having a photo does at least three things:

1. It is an *act of forthrightness* toward the people who are considering you. You can't help wondering if the person who didn't display his or her photo is hiding something.

2. It will substantially *increase the number* of contacts that you receive.

3. It will change *your mind-set from that of a fence-sitter* to that of someone who is serious and committed to online dating as a legitimate avenue to meet wonderful people.

Ladies, it is similar to when you have a boyfriend who holds your hand in public. If he does that, you know that he is really committed to the relationship, because he doesn't care about the public perception of his affection toward you. Ladies and gentlemen, having the photo up is your public display. Embrace it.

Profiles Are Organic—You Have to Tend to Them

I have also found that people's profiles evolve over time. Sometimes this is because they want to highlight a dimension that wasn't presented before but has value now. It is almost like rebaiting your hook when fishing. Sometimes, when the worm has fallen off the best position on the hook, a good fisherman pulls his pole out of the water and makes the necessary adjustments. Sometimes a fisherman will take live bait off the hook and put a synthetic worm on the line to snag the fish he desires. This ensures that his bait will attract the fish that he wants. You may have to do the same.

If you find that you are not getting enough responses, you may need to adjust or completely change your profile, including your photo. So again, don't sweat the details of your description of yourself or the description of your desired mate. You will tweak it over time. Finding your perfect match takes more than completing a questionnaire. It takes time. Whatever you do, don't exaggerate. Stick with the truth.

What Kind of Volume Should You Expect?

Once you post your profile in a decent place, you should start to receive some unsolicited contacts, which brings me to the next aspect to consider: how to think about the volume of contacts that will be generated—received or given out.

Receiving Unsolicited Contacts

Here is a common scenario. It is a typical Monday morning. It seems like a regular day. You begin at 6 AM. You work out, shower, commute to work, do some work, and commute back home. Lastly, there's dinner and a little television or reading before bed. Oh, just before you nod off, you think, "What's going on with that profile that I put up two days ago?"

So you go to your computer and check. Low and behold, you have a few messages. It is like real estate: it is working for you while you sleep. Wouldn't you know it? Someone swam past your bait and decided to take a chance and has sent you a message. Nearly a third of the contacts that I received came from unsolicited sources. Now, you have a "new" kind of choice to consider: do you open this electronic invitation with the hope of making a better acquaintance and possibly forging a real relationship, or do you just ignore it? Of course you will respond. Even though you have never met a person like this before, you are surely not going to waste the subscription fee. And you do not want the time you invested in putting the profile up in the first place to have been a waste.

Receiving unsolicited contacts is a process that is mostly out of your control. There will be peaks and troughs. Some weeks nobody will give you a holler, and then there will be weeks where you'll have to figure out what to do with the ten or more messages. A good profile will do the work necessary to bring people to you. I understand that women usually receive more unsolicited messages than men do.

Keep in mind that you cannot influence the quality of the people who send you a message. Don't fret over this, because you can't guarantee the quality of the person who approaches you at a coffee bar or anywhere people feel so compelled. I look at it as all upside: more people to consider, putting you closer to the person that you really want.

Making Contacts

Let's transition to the other method of generating leads or volume: executing your own search. This is an easy way to find the exact person that interests you, and it maintains activity in your in-box.

Creating a search is very simple. You can put just one criterion or fifteen criteria into the search request—it's up to you. If you haven't gotten comfortable with the idea of "ordering" a list of real people as though you were downloading an MP3 music file online, this feeling will subside. It is not as impersonal as you might think. You'll discover quickly that the names and photos are of real people. Like other aspects of this experience, you will refine your approach and become more sophisticated in how you utilize this tool. Sometimes you'll have a very specific query, and other times you'll execute a very broad search.

I mostly picked only profiles that had photos, and I picked a few basic criteria: height, weight, and location. I usually got a list of a few hundred people. You will find sufficient information to comb through. Imagine attempting to read two hundred or more paragraphs that describe just as many different people. You can burn through a number of hours very quickly. You actually might burn a hole in your retinas staring so long at the monitor. Occasionally, when the volume or quality of the search results was not as I had hoped, I would expand my search to include profiles without photos. This will significantly increase the number of profiles for you to consider.

The important thing here is that you do have some control. You can influence the volume that you handle by increasing or decreasing the number of unsolicited messages that you send out.

Time Does Fly—Set Limits on How Much Time You Allocate

I found myself in a certain situation several times. I'd jump online at about 9 PM on any given night. I just wanted to check my in-box at the online dating site for a half hour or so. There was usually a lot of information to go through: unsolicited new messages or replies to my previous e-mails. Often I would look up and discover that more than two hours had transpired. I certainly would not be finished. Sometimes I would feel a little exhausted and a little overwhelmed because there was so much to process.

Oftentimes I felt that I didn't want to overlook some important piece of information in someone's profile, which added to the time I spent sifting through profiles. I eventually learned that if I didn't want to permanently disrupt my evenings, I would have to become more skilled in how I spent my time going through the significant amount of information.

You will need to become skilled at sorting through the information too. Otherwise you could waste a lot of time sifting through profiles. It was something that I always had to manage. Even after becoming a veteran Internet dater, I found that this time commitment would increase whenever I joined a new Internet dating site. When I would join a new site, most of the faces were fresh, so I wanted to spend more time discovering the new folks.

I learned to set time limits. I realized that if the person was so great, that person would be there tomorrow. There was no need to spend an unhealthy amount of time looking for people to contact every evening. You have to set limits too.

The Small Things Can Make a World of Difference

Even though I had a lot of information to go through, overall I was pleased with Internet dating. I went from having no real dating activity to being a busy bee. I remember feeling a little invigorated. I thought, "Wow! I could get to know some women, and it wouldn't cost me the typical price of an apple martini that would have been necessary to initiate some conversation at a bar." It seemed like a good deal to me. All the guys can share in this benefit. Ladies, it can be beneficial for you too. At least when you tell a guy that you're not interested in him online, you don't have to look at the scowl on his face for the rest of the evening. Okay, that's it! Online dating is all about saving the cost of apple martinis and avoiding scowls. It's always the small things, right?

What Do You Do with Your List of Query Results?

Okay, you performed your search, and you got back about two hundred people, so you delve into the first ten people on the list. You look at the faces and their usernames and the first few sentences of their profiles to see if you're curious enough to view their entire profiles. Go ahead and read one of them. If you don't get a good vibe, don't waste your time. Sometimes a cursory scan is all that you need to know that the person is not the one. Move on to the next person. If you like the person and he or she seems nice, click away.

You will probably feel a little flutter in your stomach before making your initial contact. What do you say? It is best to stick with authenticity and truthfulness. Send the person a brief message indicating that you liked what you read in the profile and that you were hoping that the two of you could get to know each other a little better. Express your desire to correspond if he or she is free. You do that, and you just wait to see if the person replies. You hope that your message to them acts like a boomerang and they send a message right back to you. You want to receive a reply that reads, "Oh, you seem like a great person too, and I'm so glad that you contacted me. Let's chat further."

You can't control who will respond to your message. Don't take it as a form of personal rejection. When people drop their baited fishing lines into the water, not every fish that swims by nibbles on the bait. An entire day might go by without a response. Such is the case with sending out messages.

What Should You Do If You Don't Get an Immediate Reply?

On any given evening, you might send out two, three, or maybe four messages to new profiles. Now what do you do? You wait. You might get a reply message the same evening. It is common to receive a reply the next day. Most people who are online check their profiles at least once a day. There are people who might not check for a week or so. When I was on vacation or when I was too busy, I rarely had time to check. Generally, a day or two after you send your message, you'll know if there is interest. If it has been a week or two, just give up on that attempt and move to the next profile.

There Are Differences in the Volume for Women

I learned that women tend to have a greater volume of messages to deal with than most men do. Some Web sites allow you to see how many people have viewed a person's profile and to see how many messages a person has received. I could see that some women were receiving a tremendous volume of messages. Sometimes I saw that almost a thousand messages had been sent to some women's profiles. I remember thinking, "Wow! How in the world is this woman able to respond to a thousand messages?"

I usually avoided sending messages to those profiles. There were too many fishing poles in that small pond. Statistically speaking, it was unlikely that she would even read my message. Even if she did read my message, it was unlikely that she would respond. She had too many options. Women should avoid profiles that have an extraordinary level of activity. You are likely to get lost in the mix of messages.

One woman had written in her profile that she didn't want to waste her time and that she received too many messages. Guys who wished to send messages were instructed to make sure that they did something to impress her; otherwise she would not respond. Such an attitude can be intimidating. Most guys were never going to make it. They were going to go down like a duck sailing across the open sky in November during hunting season. Can't you smell the burning gunpowder? I could.

All of this means that to make the most of their time, women have to know what they want and be disciplined about whom they contact.

Deal with the Cold Truth—I Know That You Are Great, but Not Everyone Agrees

There's one aspect of Internet dating that you have to get used to. It holds true for us mortals. It doesn't hold true for you if people always say that you look like Beyoncé Knowles, Lucy Liu, Scarlett Johansson, Denzel Washington, George Clooney, or anybody else on America's

Most Sexy list. The truth is that, for most people, a substantial number of the initiating messages sent out will not generate a timely reply, if they generate a reply at all.

Additionally, there will be many people who will view your profile and decide not to send you a message. We do it all the time at the grocery store. We thump the cantaloupe just before we put it in the basket; if something doesn't seem right, we leave it right there and keep on walking. I know that your mom told you that you are wonderful, but not everybody thinks like mom. When you get home, you are hoping for that Tom Hanks and Meg Ryan experience in *You've Got Mail*. You send a message, and then you find the love of your life.

The reality is that a large number of people will not reply to your contacts. They may read your message and view your profile afterward but still decide not to contact you. It is par for the course. At least you can always hold on to the fact that mama still loves you. Many women didn't reply to my initial e-mails, and for sure many women who sent messages to me didn't get a reply. You have to develop thick skin.

However, there is always a profile that causes you to think, "Oh, she is the one. I know that she is Miss Right, and she is looking for me." At first, when I wouldn't get a response, I would be incensed. I was thinking, "What's up with that? I sent her a message more than three days ago. I know that she has been online to check her profile, so I know she got the message!"

It can be initially hard to adjust to the cut-and-dried aspect of Internet dating. If people aren't interested, they just aren't interested. You can't make them interested. I had to adjust, and I eventually did. Making the adjustment was a very positive thing. I just didn't need to see it as a personal repudiation. I know that you still might feel deep down that you really wanted a particular person because he was so right for you, but, again, you just have to get over it and click on the next profile. Fortunately, there are plenty of profiles. The beat goes on.

A Recap Before We Pull Up Anchor

- Focus on *brevity and being authentic*—don't overthink the profile.

- *Avoid dishonesty* and loquaciousness

- *Photos* are a must.

- Receiving contacts—*you can't control* who sends you a message.

- Making contacts—*it is easy*, and you can have it your way.

- *Set limits* on the time allocated—it can be a time drain.

- *Don't fish where everyone is fishing*—sending messages to people who have already received hundreds of messages may not be the best use of your time.

- *You are great*—not everyone is going to love you and respond to your inquiries.

- Don't take rejection personally—*mama still loves you.*

Chapter 7

Contact Management—The Two in the Two-by-Four Rule

By now, you should realize that there is a lot of potential activity that could be going on with your PC. As things get started, you'll be really excited and no doubt have a ton of energy for combing through profiles and sending and receiving messages. Don't worry—it will wear you out, and your efforts will normalize. Because you don't know who will reply to your messages and who will send you a message, you have to have a way to coordinate and orchestrate the activity. As a result, some multi-tasking will be necessary, even if you do not want to be a "player."

It Is All about the Two-by-Four Rule

During my six years of meeting and "un-meeting" people, I have discovered that there is a two-by-four rule. This has nothing to do with a plank of wood or carpentry. The two-by-four rule is a framework that I used to make sense of the people and experiences as I searched for love. In this chapter, I will elaborate on the *two* in the two-by-four rule. In the next chapter, I'll explain the *four* in the two-by-four rule.

It is unlikely that after one e-mail exchange you will decide that this person is the right person for you and that you want to establish a committed relationship. It takes about two weeks of e-mail exchange to determine whether the other person is really interested in you and whether you are really interested in the other person—hence the *two* in the two-by-four rule.

Trying to Catch a Marlin

Looking for love online reminds me of some years ago when I was deep-sea fishing with some friends off the coast of Cabo San Lucas, Mexico. We chartered a boat and drove all morning looking for "the spot" to catch a coveted marlin, one of the fiercest fish in the ocean. Just being on the water with my "boys" in pursuit of a marlin was fun enough, but yanking one out of the water would have been the cherry on top of the vacation. We had several rods in the Pacific Ocean—at least eight or so. The sun was so bright from reflecting off the ocean that it was almost blinding. We were being tossed about on the waves and baking under the midday sun.

All of a sudden we had a bite, and the game was on. We did all that we could to finesse that marlin into the boat. The experience of wrestling with this fish was exciting, but our wrestling would not guarantee that we would get the fish into the boat. We could have caught the fish, or the line could have snapped. Success or disappointment—those were our fates. It took more than a half hour of pulling, tugging, and negotiating before we got it into the boat.

Dating online is sort of like this. You have many poles in the water (i.e., e-mail messages sent to people of interest). You are not sure which one will yield anything worth your time and effort. Once you make a connection, it will take some effort before you have something real. It won't take a half hour of physically strenuous effort, but it will take time. It will take generally two weeks of communication (e-mails, phone calls, and possibly in-person interactions) before you know that you have something worth committing real time toward.

Handling Responses to Your Messages

Okay, here's how it could go. If you sent out a handful of messages the night before, you'll get one, maybe two responses. I am sure that there is some guy right now reading this and thinking, "Dude, I don't have a stick big enough to beat them back. Sometimes, I have to unplug the PC to stop the madness." Okay, this may be true for some guys or even some women. I'm really just talking to the guys and gals who have to work at it a bit.

So you open one of the responses to your message. You're excited. You begin the dialogue. The serenade begins. Usually, you'll receive a message each day from this person. Maybe you'll respond to these messages before you go to bed every night, or maybe you'll exchange a few messages during the day at work. Naturally, you are starting to get a sense of the person's personality.

Who knows? You could have a situation where you are just sitting in front of the PC and you and the other person are darting off ten or more instant messages. Don't overdo it when you start communicating with someone new. You don't want to damage a good start by being obsessed at the beginning. I never wanted to exhaust myself with one person during the initial contact.

Remember, you are not the only person that your new friend has been in contact with. Your friend doesn't want to commit all of his or her time with you initially. It is going to take more than one set of e-mail exchanges for you to have something real with this person. Engage with him or her, but let the rapport develop naturally.

Do Most Responses to E-mails Lead to Meaningful Relationships?

The answer is yes and no. It seems reasonable to think that because someone responded to your e-mail, he or she must find you interesting in some way, which improves your chances of creating a meaningful relationship. Before someone replies to a message, they will do a thorough review of the sender's profile. People oftentimes hit it off and decide to create a committed relationship. This is what you want. You want these online dating sites to improve your chances of finding someone special.

Even though finding someone special is the objective of online dating, the reality is that most of your contacts will not lead to meaningful relationships. You may have some dialogue, but it will become clear that the effort that you two are putting in should come to an end.

Why Do Most of These Contacts Come to an End?

The Reasons Are of the Standard Variety

Remember, people online are pretty much the same as those offline. Online dating helps you find people. It doesn't change the underlying nature of people. Here are a few reasons why people tend to cut folks loose:

1. The contact is a nice person but is too nice. Reading this person's messages is like reading a Hallmark card on steroids. What is that about? You can't be too nice, or you might offend? It sounds strange, but I can understand it.

2. Sometimes the topics that the person discusses just don't match what you are into (e.g., your contact talks about politics too much or how great it is to do crossword puzzles on Sunday afternoons, and you want to talk about travel or the latest reality show).

3. The comedian Chris Rock once said that a man is only as faithful as his next best option. There may be some truth to this. He may have been talking about men, but this is certainly the dynamic in online dating with both men and women during that crucial initial two-week period. Maybe while communicating with this new person, you received a message from another person who has piqued your interests more. As a result, you have to toss that first person back.

It has been less than two weeks. There wasn't much time to get to know the person.

You can't control who is sending you a message. Some people will be great, and some won't be. The great people you keep, and the others you don't.

The Market Will Have Its Way

Online dating is a social community marketplace. The mind-set is a bit like that of buyers and sellers. I experienced the harshness of the "market forces." It is all about having an appropriate matching of buyers and sellers. If you are selling something someone doesn't want to buy, there will not be a sale. If you are buying and there is a willing seller, you could have a deal.

Ladies, when that pair of shoes that you have been watching for a week or more finally goes on sale, you are all over it, right? You liked what you saw, and it was at the right price. However, if after a week of wearing them, you keep getting blisters on your heels, what are you going to do? You take those suckers back, right? Online dating is a little bit like this. After meeting someone online, if things between you don't fit, you may have to send the person back to cyberspace. The market will determine what goods get bought and sold.

How Are These Encounters Brought to an End?

A lot of people will meet one another online, and not everyone will like everyone else, so there has to be an effective way to end things. Just as people may want to end things with you after several days of communicating, you will want to have that same level of control if you think things aren't going well.

Having an online profile is like sleeping with the front door of your house wide open. Anybody can walk in. You may want some people to stay. Other people walk in uninvited, and you want them to go. You invited some of the others, but nevertheless you want them to go too.

You just have to know the correct way to ask people to leave when you don't want them there. You could tell them, "Hey, I think that you are great, but I don't think that we should continue to exchange messages; I wish you well in your search." That would be the nice and polite thing to do, right? I tried this approach initially. I found out that people tend to do things differently.

She Wiggled out of My Hands—Was It Something I Said?

Have you ever seen a segment from one of those "funniest home video" programs where a guy holds a large fish that he has just pulled out of the water? He is inspecting it and has a glow of pride as he displays it on camera. Then, all of a sudden, the fish unleashes a vigorous wiggle in order to free itself and return to the sea. We have seen this type of clip often. It is a classic gaffe. The fish had determined that it was not going to be a fillet that day. As quickly as the man possessed the fish, he was left empty-handed, wondering what had happened.

In the first couple weeks after making a contact with people, a portion of them will suddenly disappear from you too. When this first happened to me, I was left to wonder whether it was something that I had said. In one moment, I was trying to establish something with a lady. I was spilling my guts about what I thought was important to me in life. Then, in the next moment, I was left high and dry. I was in an echo chamber. The only voice I heard was my own. I was just baffled.

I thought that things were going okay. Then there was nothing. I hadn't received any reply messages back from her, so I checked her profile to see if she had logged on. To my dismay, yes, she had logged on. This meant that she was fully aware of the messages I'd sent. At first I thought, "How could she dis me like that?" I would check my e-mails and my profile two or three days in a row to see if I had gotten a message from this person just to see if she had changed her mind. I was hoping that she would make contact again. I felt that I had to make sure.

I eventually realized that I didn't want to make contact with her necessarily to salvage the little bit of relationship that we'd started but simply to ask her why she went silent that way. You know how people are: when there is a breakup, the person who is taken by surprise always wants to know why.

I knew that with online dating, at some point, someone would stop expressing interest in me and decide to stop contacting me. In my imagination, I must have deluded myself into thinking that it would end gently, like this: "Hey, you are a great guy, and I am almost in love with you and could imagine you as the father of my children, but I just got transferred to the Philippines for my job. Let's not put ourselves through the hardship of such a long-distance relationship." Even though the answer may have been bogus, at least it would have been a clear indication that it was over.

The abrupt silence made it seem as if the e-mail exchange never really occurred. As abruptly as it became real, it became unreal. It was as if someone had taken a pencil with an eraser and just erased the fact that this person and I had ever talked about how great we both were and how much we had in common.

It was apparent, in retrospect, that I was such a *neophyte* about this. The truth was that she had made her decision to move on and that I needed to move on too. After a few more incidents of shock and disappointment like this, I realized that this was the way the game was played.

This abrupt disconnect happened to me regularly, and it will happen to you. People don't have time or patience for elaborate good-byes if they have talked to you for only three days.

You Will Have to Toss Back a Number of Fish

When you're fishing, you soon realize that not every catch is worth taking back home to cook. Some of the fish will be too small. Some of the fish will be unsightly. You won't want to eat these creatures. Consequently, you have to toss them back. The same is true after you meet someone online. Just as some people lost interest in you and wiggled free, you'll have to toss back some of those guys and gals that you thought were great initially.

After you have made your first e-mail exchange, you'll have contact with him or her at varying levels. It depends on the chemistry. Before the two-week mark, things can go many different ways. Maybe it is day five, and you just are a little tired of communicating with this person. Who knows why? It doesn't really matter. You like him as a person but not enough to continue to sink more time into getting to know him. It is not very sensitive to use the word *sink* as if the other person isn't someone with feelings, but you are wasting time with this person if you know that things should not go much further. Here's what happened to me when I had to toss back some fish.

Giving Long Explanations Every Time Became a Bit Difficult

When the shoe was on the other foot, I had learned to respect and appreciate the free market aspect of starting and ending contacts with people online. Just as there were women who summarily ended things with me, I found that I needed to find an effective way to move on as well. It quickly became exhausting to tell every woman with whom I had lost interest that I no longer wanted to exchange e-mails. Turning down people is something that you will do more frequently. It is a tacit form of rejection, though people shouldn't take it too personally. You don't want to hurt people's feelings, but because you are going to meet many more people online than you have time for, you will have to become comfortable with turning down more people than you may be used to.

The Gentle and Detailed Way

When I felt that it was time to end things, some women were good about what was likely unavoidable. The moment would come when I didn't want to continue communicating. Initially, I had a detailed and gentle way of explaining that it was over. I would explain that she was nice but that we should both move forward—however, move forward separately. I would wish her well in her search. I hoped that she would understand and move on.

Some would thank me for being honest and not wasting their time. Then, of course, there were the ones who couldn't understand why the contacts should end. It would become a big incident, even though we had exchanged e-mails for only a week. Some of the women made it seem as if we were soul mates. In my mind, I was like, "Dang, let it go; it ain't that serious. It has only been seven days."

I Had to Adjust My Ways

After having to face several of these adverse reactions, it became clear that I had to employ the "abrupt silence" approach that I was experiencing from women. In fact, it made things much more efficient. Occasionally, I would give a woman a much more elaborate reason why we needed to end things. That usually happened if we'd spent more than a week or so exchanging e-mails. I am usually not a fan of doing what everyone else does, but I can understand why a large number of online daters feel the need to toss people back using the "abrupt silence" termination method.

You Have to Have More Than One Fishing Pole in the Water

There will be a high turnover in contacts. You can't place all of your hopes in the one person that responds to your e-mail. People are going to be wiggling out of your hands, and you will be tossing people back with regularity. Some of those contacts will last for one day, some will last for one week, and some will actually last to the point where you might want to start something meaningful with the person. You just don't know. Consequently, you have to have more fishing poles in the water.

Your profile is a fishing pole in the water. The e-mails that you send out are fishing poles in the water. You want people to respond to your profile, and you want people to respond to your e-mails. People with a pole in the water have no certainty that they will catch a fish, but you have to have a pole in the water to catch a fish. If you catch a fish, you may have to toss it back, or it could wiggle out of your hands. Likewise, once you make contact with someone, whether he or she contacted you by looking at your profile or you contacted him or her with an e-mail, there is no certainty that after a few days or weeks this person not will wiggle free or you will not toss him or her back.

You could toss them all back, and they may all wiggle free in the same week, which is why you have to have multiple fishing poles in the water in order to keep the pipeline fed.

You May Have Something Real at Two Weeks

Oh, but if you can make it to two weeks, you just might have something. After two weeks, you'll know whether you are getting a good vibe. You will have learned a fair amount about this person, and he or she will have learned a lot about you. If the other person is not interested, he or she will have wiggled free by then.

I would wait as long as reasonably possible before you meet in person. Don't invest time unless you get a good feeling about the person. Otherwise, you are practically going on a blind date. If you make it to two weeks, you may not have the love of your life, but then again you might. Beyond two weeks, there is a greater chance that the contact will develop into a girlfriend or a boyfriend. Even if you don't decide to meet the contact after two weeks, you will probably have a strong desire to continue the e-mails.

The longer you maintain contact with someone, the less likely he or she is to abruptly disappear. Once you have something more meaningful, the traditional relationship skills should kick in. Remember, you are still dealing with human beings who are unpredictable, so after two weeks you will probably do yourself a service by keeping your expectations in check and letting the relationship develop as any other relationship would.

A Recap Before We Pull Up Anchor

- The *two-by-four framework* will help you make sense of contact management.

- It takes about *two weeks of regular and meaningful communication* with someone before you have something worth putting solid time toward.

- *You won't* like everyone, and *not everyone will* like you.

- Some people who seem like a catch will *wiggle free*.

- Some people who seemed like a catch to you will have to be *tossed back*.

- If the contact is less than two weeks old and there was little communication, an *abrupt silence and a ceasing* of contact means that it is over; people will use this approach, and you should too.

- Keep *several poles* in the water.

Chapter 8

Contact Management—The Four in the Two-by-Four Rule

Four Is Company; More Is a Crowd—The Four *in* the Two-by-Four Rule

As you go through the process of figuring out who might be the right person for you, you have to remember that there will be more than one person giving you a once-over. A critical question that you may ask during this process is, "How many people can I communicate with at one time?" Because of the turnover during the first two weeks, you should definitely focus on more than one person. Otherwise, you will go through repeated and discouraging periods of inactivity. Okay, now that you know that you should have more than one person, you should let it rip, right? Should you have five, ten, fifteen, or twenty contacts?

Here's the deal. You should not attempt to nurture contacts with more than four people at one time. You can be in contact with less than four individuals but not more than four. In the previous chapter, I discussed three things that affect the number of contacts that you can communicate with at any given time:

1. You can't control who is going to send you a message, and you can't determine who will respond to your messages. The volume could be high at times.

2. You can't expect to have something that is "real" until you have reached the two-week mark, which means that you have to put in time. You have a limited amount of time to allocate to a limited number of people.

3. Because of the short duration of encounters, people will be coming in and out of your online experience, so you have to keep the pipeline fed. This can be too tricky to handle if you try to take on too many contacts.

All three of these conditions make it clear that you will have a large number of contacts. You want to know how to manage the volume. It doesn't matter to which online dating site you subscribe: eHarmony, Match.com, MySpace.com, or any other. The dynamics that I am highlighting are human behavioral tendencies, which are independent of any service provided to assist in finding love. You don't want an overflow or a dearth of prospects. You want to manage your experience as reasonably as possible.

Four Has Always Worked for Us in Other Areas

The number four has worked for us in several areas in life. For example, when traveling with friends, it is always better to go in a group of no more than four people. That fifth person will feel like the odd man out, making things seem out of balance. Have you ever tried to fit three of the five people in the backseat of a sedan during a ten-hour road trip? I can tell you that the folks in the back are not too pleased. You know as well as I do that trying to get five or six people to agree on anything can be too painful. Four is a bit more manageable.

The same value of four holds for managing online dating. Experience has shown me time and time again that the maximum number of dialogues that one should try to maintain is four; this is enough to ensure that a person is adequately busy but not too busy and certainly not bored. If you go for more than four, you could find yourself in a little trouble.

The Weekly Volume of Contacts Will Fluctuate

Because of the *two* in the two-by-four rule, I found myself having really interesting conversations for just about two weeks or shorter. Something would happen, and then either I would disappear or she would disappear, which is why maintaining more than one dialogue was important. Additionally, because the responses to my initiating e-mails could be intermittent, I had to have a way to preserve the flow. There were always potential contacts from the unsolicited e-mails. You couldn't control this volume.

During some weeks, more than half of the women would respond to my messages, and I would have a load of information to manage; then there would be periods that were dry. I mean as dry as an elbow under a wool sweater during the depths of winter. There would be nothing—nada. No love or even a hint of love could be found. It is like a fisherman who tosses a net over the side of the boat, looking to make a good catch. Sometimes the net comes back full of tasty fish, and sometimes the net is empty and just full of old beat-up cans. Just as the quantity of e-mails can vary, the quality of the e-mails that you receive can vary just as greatly. The varying quality of the contacts that you make underscores the importance of having multiple contacts but not more than four.

As the volume of contacts fluctuates, so does the amount of information associated with all of these people. You are effectively maintaining a system of rotation. People will rotate into your four, and people will rotate out. You can't remember everything, so you have to set limits. It is much easier to remember the details of four people than it is to remember the details of eight people.

You Are Sort of Like a Coach

In basketball, there are twelve men on a team, but only five players make the starting rotation. These players most closely match what the coach is looking for. Over a season, the people who make up the five-man rotation can change. Someone could get injured or play poorly and get pulled from the stating lineup. Other prospects defy expectations and perform surprisingly well, which persuades the coach to change the starting five in the rotation. A coach has to be attentive to maintaining a good balance. A coach can't try to play all twelve players. That is just not effective, and it will overwhelm the coach's ability to be successful. The same is true for you. If you try to manage an inordinately large number of contacts, you will not be successful in finding a good partner.

In a sense, adhering to the *four* in the two-by-four rule is like being a basketball coach who is constantly looking for four people to fill the open rotation spots. I usually used this rotation approach when I was dealing with a group of women with whom I had not yet reached the two-week mark. People will be voluntarily and involuntarily leaving the rotation. You just want to try to maintain the balance

How Do You Determine Who Makes the Four-Spot Rotation?

The quality of the person should drive your decisions regarding the makeup of your rotation. When I mention quality, I am not talking about a person's "Hollywood" quality, the superficial stuff. It really doesn't have anything to do with physical characteristics per se. Physical traits are hopefully just one item on your list of criteria. It is about trying to match your wants to the right set of people. Finding someone who meets your criteria goes a long way to improving the likelihood of relationship success. A quality response comes from someone who comes fairly close to the criteria that you specified in your profile.

If you are a woman who indicated that you were looking for a male between twenty-five and thirty years of age, of medium build, who has never married, who has no children, and who lives within twenty-five miles from your home, but you receive an e-mail from a man who describes himself in his profile as forty years of age, divorced with two children, and residing fifteen hundred miles away, my opinion is that this person represents a lower-quality e-mail. You should not respond to this e-mail. It doesn't matter what he looks like.

You have to know what you want from the beginning and stick to the criteria.

Look for What You Want

From what I have heard from the women that I have met, their mail-boxes are littered weekly with these sorts of mismatched e-mails. Maybe you are open to being very flexible with your selection criteria. That's fine. But just know that initiating contact with someone who is a poor fit substantially reduces your chances for success and is not the best use of your time.

Whatever your criteria, you can enforce them without engaging in a conversation and possibly two or three months of dates before you realize that this person hates playing Scrabble, hates watching *The Sopranos*, and considers himself or herself very serious and matter-of-fact, all of which are the opposite of how you would describe your ideal mate. Establishing criteria doesn't guarantee success, but it certainly helps narrow down the field of contenders.

This Is Not a Cloaked Effort to Sanction Playing the Field

I hope no one is thinking, "Oh, he is just a guy who wants to be a player." I am not suggesting that people throw out their commitment to fidelity. The *four* in the two-by-four rule creates the conditions that allow you to get to know several people simultaneously while offering the flexibility to deal with the unpredictable attitudes and interests of the people you meet online during the first two weeks of contact.

I was too busy with life to actually have more than one "real" relationship at a time. I'm talking about a real relationship in which two people go out on dates and see each other with some regularity and commitment. Most of the contacts that you make will be temporary and will lack commitment.

Everyone is free to engage with other folks as they see fit. My recommendation is to apply the two-by-four rule; then, once you have found someone that you like you, you can begin to focus on that person in a more dedicated way.

Is It Easy to Get to Know Four People Simultaneously?

You imagine sending and receiving e-mails with ease. You hit your groove. People are taking the bait that your profile offers. People are also wiggling free, and you are tossing some back. You are sure that you will get thick-skinned about the Machiavellian tempo of the online space. However, you wonder, "Is it difficult to possibly get to know four people at one time?" Sometimes it can be. People are not very easy to put into a formula. This certainly holds true when dealing with multiple people, simultaneously.

You may have added all of these new people to the rotation on the same day or the same night, or you may have added one person a day for four days or some strange combination in between. Who knows? The point is that not only will you probably meet them at different moments, if not on different days, but your relationships with them will most likely progress at different paces. So, yes, it can be difficult, but I have some thoughts that will make it easier.

Coordination of Information Is Essential

We have all played this game with friends. We discover that we are not very coordinated as we attempt to rub our stomachs while simultaneously patting the tops of our heads. It is more challenging than you might think. Keeping some order to the people in your rotation is sort of like this. At times, it can be difficult to maintain the balance.

Coordinating information is the biggest challenge. With some people, things go smoothly from the beginning. With others, things can progress a bit more methodically. The contacts that progress more slowly require more time. I found that in order to make all my inter-actions feel authentic, I would selectively go back and reread each person's previous message to reacquaint myself with not only what the person was talking about but also the tone and feel of the conversa-tion. Most times it wasn't that prescriptive. You will have to do this sometimes if you have four contacts that are progressing much more slowly. You don't want to refer to the dominance of the New York Yankees when the other person has already indicated how much he or she loves the Boston Red Sox, the Yankees' bitter rival. That kind of mix-up will create unintended awkwardness.

Some people might say, "Well, if you were really interested in the person, you would not need to have multiple people with whom to correspond." There is some truth to this, but keep in mind that every-one I was still conversing with had been around for less than the two weeks. Really, I didn't know them very well. They didn't know me either, so it was not too wise to become singularly committed in the initial days. I was still sniffing things out, gathering information.

Maintaining Multiple Contacts Is Like Cooking a Meal without Burning It

There were times when I felt as if I needed to be a master chef, main-taining multiple simmering pots without burning the Sunday dinner. Each dish needed its specialized recipe. Each person in your four-per-son rotation is different, and you need to engage with each person in unique and specific ways. I needed to nurture each dialogue appropri-ately to see if there was really something there.

For those who watch one or several of the cooking shows on cable tele-vision, imagine you are one of the highly skilled cooks. They are cooking Chilean sea bass, making some exotic potato dish, and preparing some fancy vegetable appetizer. They always seem to have a blowtorch ready to caramelize something. The process always seems skilled and under control. There's no sweat, no dishes are broken, and certainly no meals are burned. It all is working together. The last thing that the chef wants is for something to burn.

That is the kind of harmony that I was trying to maintain. Generally, that was how it worked out. I tried to maintain no more than four contacts at any given time. Can you imagine cooking a meal for a larger group with ten dishes, simultaneously? I can imagine disaster in the future for anyone attempting such a feat. Disaster may also be your destination if you get too aggressive with the number of people you try to maintain at one time. Be disciplined. It will serve you well.

A Recap Before We Pull Up Anchor

- The *two-by-four framework* will help you make sense of contact management.

- Maintain *no more than four contacts* at any given time.

- People will be coming in and going out of your online experience, so *maintaining the four-person rotation* is an important requirement.

- Because contacts evolve at their own pace, *coordination of information* is the most challenging aspect of nurturing four distinct contacts.

Chapter 9

Sticking to the Four in the Two-by-Four Rule
Two Ways to Burn a Meal

1. Nurturing Too Many Contacts Simultaneously Will Burn a Meal

Forget Gordon Gecko from the movie *Wall Street*. Greed is not good. Too much of most things will usually create some undesired outcome. The same holds true with online dating. There is a reason why there is a *four* in the two-by-four rule.

Sure, there are some people who are better than most in skillfully nurturing more than four active dialogues over a period of time. Some people like a little risk. For the average person, my original direction stands. After your four rotation spots have been filled, *stop sending messages*! I'm telling you, if you have more than four moderately engaging conversations going on at once, it will all start to become a blur. You won't be able to keep track of what has been going on in the lives of the various people. Sooner or later, usually sooner, you will be exposed. If you violate this principle, you will be in the fast lane headed for the destination called disaster. Your flub will send you careening out of control.

Here's What Happened When I Violated My Own Rule

Experience Is the Best Teacher

It was unfortunate to have dealt with the consequences of my own greed. At least you can benefit from what I learned. I was a few years into online dating. I was what you might call "seasoned." I had had a number of online relationships of varying lengths. I had gotten comfortable, or one might say "skilled," enough to maintain activity on two or three dating sites at the same time. There were at least two or three active discussions that I had going on within each site at any given time. Here I was violating the *four* in my two-by-four rule. Every night, I would have at least one or two e-mails from the different ladies. I seemed to be handling the six to nine dialogues fine. Experience would show me that following well-thought-out rules was the better option.

I Think I Was Having a Senior Moment

All seemed to be going well, until my overextended but smoothly running rotation began to get out of balance. I started to get an inordinate number of messages from one woman who seemed to be increasingly indicating her interest in me. Even though I had six to nine people in my rotation, women were still wiggling free, and I was tossing some back. It was nice to see one of the contacts start to blossom. This was just what I was looking for, right? Obviously, I felt that she met a lot of my basic criteria. That's why we were conversing. There was one problem, and it was growing with every passing day.

Here was the situation. I had been in light dialogue with multiple women for more than two or three weeks. This particular woman, who was showing increased interest, lived in another town, so I had never met her in person, but the dialogue was very healthy. We were sharing more and more information. The problem with my interactions with this really lovely woman was that I could not remember her name! I couldn't believe it. I found a woman who was really interested in me, and I was starting to really enjoy our conversations. How could I forget her name?! I was too young to start forgetting things. When you get older, it is understandable that you may forget a few things, but it shouldn't happen to someone in his mid-thirties. Was I having a "senior" moment?

Be Suspicious If the Other Person Never Uses Your Name in Messages

She was so sweet and well intentioned when she ended her e-mails. Her e-mails would end like this: "Well, it was nice to speak to you again, Myles. I hope that you have a great day. I look forward to your next message, hugs …" She would also end the message with one of those Internet text smiles with the colon, dash, and right parenthesis: :-). I would be filled with mixed emotions. I would think, "Wow, she seems really nice." But then I would think, "What in the world is her name?" That would just make me feel anxious. I was afraid that one day she might get suspicious about the fact that I never used her name when I ended my messages to her.

When you belong to an organization where you see people with regularity (e.g., work, school, church, Internet dating site), sometimes it can be difficult to remember everyone's name. I have been in this position before, and I suspect that most people have too. There is always someone who remembers your name after you are introduced, and for the life of you, you can't remember that person's name. The person says very confidently, "Hey, Lisa!" and is practically waving with both hands as she calls your name. You draw a mental blank because you don't remember the overly enthused person's name. The voice in your head is franticly running through a list of names, hoping to find the right one. "Leslie? No. Linda? No. Shoot!" This woman is moving in fast to give you a hug, so you flash one of those million-dol-lar smiles and reply, "Heeeeey." You try to beat it out of there as fast as possible before you are discovered.

That is how I felt every time this unnamed woman sent me a mes-sage. That same voice in my head was running through a list of names, hoping to find the right one. I thought that it would be better to send messages without a name instead of guessing wrong. Maybe I would remember her name later, I reasoned.

The Consequences of Greed Had Come to Torment Me

Satisfaction and anxiety—those were my daily emotional allotments every time I got a message from her. My own name, Myles, would torment me and echo in my head every time I read her messages. It would echo because it was a resounding reminder of the fact that she liked me enough to remember my name, but I couldn't remember her name. I at least had several photos that helped me to visualize the author of these nice messages, but none of them were helpful in stir-ring my memory of her name. I was being menaced by my own name. I desperately searched my personal e-mail mailbox for older e-mails that she had sent, hoping to find one with her name in it.

I realized that she must have told me her name in the first e-mail that she sent. The problem for me was that she had sent it two to three weeks before, and I had deleted that e-mail. Seems like the normal thing to do, right? In addition, my mailbox was a bit full. Remember, I was in the midst of my greed fest. I was maintaining conversations with six to nine people at one time, which can generate a lot of sent and received messages. I was trying to keep my in-box manageable.

One lesson learned was that I should not have deleted any of them just for the sake of organization. Sure, many of those interactions/conversations would die an early and natural death, but until then I should have kept the old e-mails. When you get greedy, you get care-less, which can lead to problems that can torment you.

The Jig Was Up

So what happened? Well, I realized that I couldn't carry on like that. I was starting to enjoy the conversations with this woman even more. She was also beginning to really like a guy who couldn't remember her name. What was I going to do, wait until the marriage ceremony for the pastor to say her name during the repeating of the marriage vows for me to relearn her name? No way. Based on how I handled this situation, I wouldn't have made it that far anyway. I had to face this dilemma straight on. The jig was up—no more hiding in the shadows of my error.

It took me a moment or two to select the correct words for the e-mail, but I had to tell her. I was really embarrassed, but I had to be honest with her or risk causing even more pain. I told her that I had forgotten her name and that I had deleted the one message in which she had communicated it to me. I tried to explain how sorry I was and how difficult it was to ask her for her name again. This explanation did not vindicate me in her eyes. Once the discussion was over, it became clear that she was not pleased.

Once You Are Tossed Back, Your Chance Is Over

Okay, I was clearly in the wrong for not being more careful and for not following my own advice. I thought that maybe it would blow over, but she employed the infamous "abrupt silence" method of dealing with a careless person such as me. She went radio silent like nobody's business. I had been tossed back. I never heard from her again. I sent a few messages to try to reignite things, but I am sure that those messages were shot down by her delete button. Her feelings were probably a little hurt, but given the nature of Internet dating, she probably had three other pots on the stove, so I didn't feel too bad; however, I should have been more careful, and so should you.

The Moral of This Story

What can you learn from this experience? There is a reason why principles are useful. They are generally effective, so try to follow them. It will be fun to meet so many new and interesting people. With each person you add, the more complex it becomes, and the more likely you are to make the kind of error that I made. Don't let greed get the best of you.

Another Way That You Can Burn a Meal

2. Being a Chatty Kathy—Too Many Simultaneous Instant Message Conversations

In addition to the standard process of exchanging e-mails, many people utilize instant messaging to quickly have a dialogue. The rhythm of instant message (IM) conversations is very fluid. It is almost like speaking with the person. Sometimes when you are instant messaging with someone, another person will notice that you are in an active chat and will send you an IM.

Instant Message Interruptions

Often dating sites will include an indicator on the Web page that will let people know your status as they view your profile. They know if you are active on the site, if you are sending and viewing messages, or even if you are in an IM conversation. It can be useful, but I found that it really does remove a layer of privacy and discretion.

So here you are having an IM conversation or sending an e-mail, and then, bam, another person sends you an IM. Some people think that if you are in IM with someone, you are available to have a conversation with them. That may be true sometimes but not always. When this happened to me, it presented a dilemma. One option was to ignore this person's message to me, which I thought was not ideal, because this person already knew that I was conversing with someone else, so it would be a flagrant hand-to-the-face rejection. The other option was to start a conversation with this new person while still in conversation with the original person.

Again, the Challenge of Managing Volume

As you might imagine, this required a decent amount of concentration. It was like trying to have a twenty-minute conversation on the phone with two different people on a two-way line. It's even more difficult to maintain three conversations on a three-way line. With all of the clicking back and forth and the other person or people waiting for you to respond, it can be stressful for everyone.

If I was in an IM conversation with two people, I found it a bit challenging but manageable when they were asking really short questions that required quick responses. I had to be really quick in my typing. The situation was made infinitely more complex when I was trying to maintain at least two IM conversations with a quick question/response tempo while simultaneously having a third IM conversation with another person who asked detailed questions that required longer and more meaningful answers. These conversations progressed at different speeds, so it got tough quick.

The other people would ask a series of simple questions like, "What time are you going to the movies?" Then that question would be followed up with, "Who are you going with?" and so forth. They were just short fact-gathering questions. It was difficult to answer these questions quickly enough and still focus and respond to the more substantial question from the other person. Many times, I would have to break off from typing a long response just to type a one-word answer for the quick-tempo dialogues to buy some time to complete the more detailed answer. There was a string of no, yes, and maybe answers.

What was ideal for me was when there were two people who wanted to have substantive conversations. I could give detailed answers to both people, and if it took a little while, neither person was bothered, because my answers were thoughtful and would naturally take more

time to construct. However, neither of them knew that I was fever-
ishly typing these detailed answers.

Arrogance and Then the Fall, Again

Generally, the physical requirement of switching from one person to
another was fairly easy. You just click one icon for May's dialogue and
quickly click Cynthia's icon in order to continue with her. Of course,
like all processes where we get too comfortable, we tend to get used
to them and possibly a little careless. That is what I did in trying to
maintain simultaneous IM conversations. I felt that I could handle this
environment without much difficulty, because I had done this several
times before. But as the saying goes, "Pride comes before the fall."
What did I do? I did what any person who was just a little too self-
assured would do: I pushed the limits and let greed creep in again.

Soon I was maintaining four or five IM conversations simultaneously. I was a little impressed with my ability to surf the Net and check
world news, talk on the phone, and maintain four different IM conversations simultaneously. It was a little insane, but it was working.
Well, it was working until I was "called out" by a woman who was getting the short end of the stick. I wasn't getting back to her fast enough
with my responses.

She simply got fed up and told me, "Look, if you don't want to talk
to me and you want to talk to other people, fine. I have to go." *Click.*
That was it. She signed off. This was another instance when I was
tossed back. I felt terrible. I'll admit that I was becoming a little crazed
by the practice that I had started.

What Did I Learn from Excessive IMs?

From that point on, I decided to have no more than two IM conversations at one time and preferably only one. If someone sent me a
request for an IM conversation and I already had two conversations
going, I ignored that person's request or told them that I'd try them

later. I usually took note of their profile name and sent them a message later if I had interest.

The lesson learned was that Chatty Kathy, namely me, needed to be less chatty.

A Recap Before We Pull Up Anchor

- Maintaining *no more than four contacts* in your rotation can reduce the potential for *embarrassment.*

- *Excessive instant messaging* can become challenging to manage.

- Try not to have more than *two IM conversations* going at a given time.

Chapter 10

What People Say Means Something

Spending six years learning a new way to meet people gave me an opportunity to discover some interesting lessons. One of them is that you should pay attention to what people say, because it says a lot about them.

The Three Rs—Well, at Least Two

Reading and writing are fundamental. *When were reading and writing ever a prerequisite for dating?*

You will likely recall from your childhood days how any school worth anything stressed the importance of the Big Three. They were the three Rs: reading, writing, and arithmetic. Every child with hopes of being a productive member of this society needed to master the Big Three. It still doesn't make sense to me why they call them the three Rs. Only one of the words starts with an *R*. It appears to have worked, because most people remember the three Rs long after they finish school. When I started dating online, I soon realized how extensively my writing skills needed to be used. Looking back, it was more than I expected.

People's Writing Skills on Full Display

Well, as much as people remember the principle of the three Rs, not everyone is as adept at reaching back to all that they learned. It was amazing to read the number of profiles that had a phenomenal number of misspellings and grammatical no-nos. This lack of written proficiency could be a by-product of the twenty-first century and the e-mail age.

How many people have received e-mails from coworkers or class-mates that are filled with so many grammatical holes that the messages resemble Swiss cheese? I'm not talking about the efficient e-mail slang or abbreviations such as *lol*, which means "laugh out loud," usually used to let the other person know that you think that whatever just happened was really funny. I'm talking about just plain carelessness. Who knows? Maybe the Internet has revealed that the world's educational systems aren't as good as we might think, and all of our short-comings are being put on full display before all who would receive a message or read our profiles.

Make Your First Impression a Good One

Heck, I can empathize a bit with those careless typists. I have been one of them. Even though I try to use spell-check before I send out some-thing, every now and again I slip up, and upon rereading the message I wonder what I was thinking when I wrote that note. If you start out communicating with someone and you receive these kinds of e-mails, it is easy to form a slightly negative impression of the other person. It is not a deal breaker, but it does become one strike against that person. I am certainly not a literary or grammatical snob. I am hardly Frasier Crane.

My advice is that you should pay attention to the quality of your communications, particularly in your first few communications, because first messages are lasting. Be thoughtful, proofread, and use spell-check.

What and How Someone Says Something Says a Lot

Friends would often ask me how I was able to really get to know the nature of a person through e-mails and IMs. Over time, I began to see two consistencies from the profiles that I read and the e-mails that I received:

1. An individual's personality can be identified from how the person describes himself or herself.

2. The manner in which a person corresponds via e-mails is a strong indicator for how that person will verbally communicate with you.

Reading the Personality from the Profile

When a guy describes himself as someone who likes watching the X Games, snowboarding, and traveling to Vegas to play in poker tournaments, you can get a pretty good idea of what kind of person he is.

Of course, you won't know for sure until you spend more time getting to know him, but he obviously is a physically active person, possibly athletic in build. He is a risk taker and probably very confident. He is a thinker, because he likes to compete in poker. He may even be a little overconfident. This guy likes to wager his body and his money. You may wonder about his sense of responsibility, but it is still too early to know. His profile might be a little scary for you, or he might be just what you are looking for.

When a woman describes herself in the following way, you can very quickly get a sense of her personality: "I am someone who loves being in the water. I like being outdoors in just about any season. I really enjoy hiking, playing volleyball, traveling, and anything that involves activity. I love great food, and great conversations with friends are my passions. I oftentimes talk with my hands. Sometimes watching me is like watching a traffic cop work his way through rush hour traffic (smile)." I would imagine that she has a prominent and engaging personality and that she has a lot of energy. Depending on what you are looking for, she could be worth the follow-up or she might be too intense for you.

From each of these descriptions, the words that people communicate are the windows through which you can begin to see who they are as people. These words are enough for you to start assessing whether they are a good fit for you.

How Something Is Said Is as Important as What Is Said

I'm not talking about grammar here. I'm talking about whether people use "high" English to describe themselves or whether they drape themselves in excessive slang and colloquial phrases. The main point here is to go with the person that fits your style. Usually, people with similar communication styles can understand each other better, even the nuances. There are times when you could be looking for something different.

I met a woman once online who spoke in so much slang that I had to ask her to not speak it so much, because I felt that she was trying too hard. She was telling me that I was trippin', and she was like, "Yo, that was crazy phat." I was thinking to myself, "What in the world is going on here?" I thought that I was going to have to throw down some gang signs to be legit with her. Her slang was so frequent that it was almost not genuine. I understood her completely, but I wasn't turned on by how she communicated things to me. I guess she was hoping that I would either join in or be okay with her style. Neither was the case. This disconnect, among other things, caused me to end the contacts with her. The communication just wasn't great.

I was a bit confused by the experience because of how her behavior and mannerisms were disconnected from her photo. There usually is a tremendous amount of congruence in how people describe themselves, their style of communication, and their photos. If he look like a strait-laced, moderate guy but starts talking like he just finished five years in the San Quentin penitentiary, alarm bells should go off. Unfortunately, this was the case with the hip-hop soul sista that I mentioned earlier.

She presented herself physically in a straightforward manner. There were no Crips' or Bloods' bandanas. Unfortunately, her physical appearance belied her communication style, which was a turnoff for me.

The Truth Will Set You Free

As you might suspect, everybody ain't tellin' the truth online. This is probably one of the most common things that people think of when you mention Internet dating—everyone is lying. The truth is, most people are being honest, but for sure there are some bona fide liars out there. Let me share with you an experience that I had with a woman who was deceptive.

How I Almost Became the "Other Guy" for Somebody's Wife

I can remember once when a woman contacted me via one of the mainstream dating sites. It appeared that she was really interested in getting to know me. Her profile indicated that she was single. Her general description of herself was appealing, so I felt that it would be worthwhile to start having conversations with her. She was in the rotation. Everything was going fine until about two weeks into it. Remember the *two* in the two-by-four rule? We were both still trying to see if what we had was "real."

Even though I assumed that she had been honest with me from the start, I guess at a certain point she decided that she was going to be more forthright with me. Being forthright is always a good thing. The problem was that I had assumed that she was already being completely forthright. People turn from the untruth to the truth for a lot of reasons. For her, maybe it was because she was really starting to like me. Things were going really well. We had not met in person at this point, but our e-mail exchanges were frequent and engaging.

Well, she disclosed that she was not, in fact, single but had been married for three years. She was hoping that I would take solace in her admission because she was having long-term challenges with her.

husband. With her marriage on the rocks, she felt that it was a good time to establish a relationship with another man. You know, I was sorry to hear about her failing relationship, but come on now. I was thinking, "Why are you dragging me into your situation? You're just creating a mess!"

I was annoyed because she had lied and because the nature of her untruth was not trivial. I was almost an adulterer. Just think if things had gone further. I would have been entangled with a woman who was legally and emotionally committed to another man. The impending love triangle involving her, me, and the understandably jealous husband was something that I had no desires to sign up for. Consequently, I had to bring our budding romance to an end. I had to toss her back.

Some People Pretend to Be Other People

A slight exaggeration is not the same as a complete fabrication. I also remember that I met a woman who sent me a message from some small country in Europe. She had indicated that she was working as a professional in the medical field as an administrator, but as the days went on I came to discover that she was not exactly who she was pretending to be.

It turned out that she was from Boston and was an American. She had not gotten a graduate degree and wasn't working in the medical field. I was thinking, "Who are you then?" If I was going to get to know her, I was going to have to start over. She apologized for not telling the truth. I was not too annoyed by it, because it had only been about three days. However, I was thinking, "What motivates a person to pretend to be someone else?"

Some people exaggerate a bit. We are all familiar with that. When a guy says that he is six feet tall but is really five feet nine and a half inches, that is exaggeration. Creating an entirely untrue personality profile requires different motivations. After she disclosed her true identity, I didn't hear from her again. I think she was embarrassed about lying.

Honesty Is Far Better

I am sure that several women can empathize. Men have also played this same game of bait and switch. Even though people communicate certain things in their profiles and in their e-mails, it is possible that they are not telling the truth. Lying is an unavoidable aspect of the human condition. This was true before the Internet and is true now with online dating. Most people are honest, but just know that some people are not representing themselves accurately.

So, yes, people sometimes lie, but I don't think dishonesty is any more widespread online than it is in the "real" world. My advice here is for you to convey the truth. Lying usually isn't a great way to start out a friendship or significant relationship. Honesty is a much easier proposition to maintain. Hey, if they don't like you after you have been honest, then let them wiggle free. You will have more time for people who are interested and honest with you. If you find someone lying in a major way in the early part of the discussions, don't waste time. Cut them loose, and toss them back. As they say, there are plenty of fish in the sea.

A Recap Before We Pull Up Anchor

- *Writing skills are now a significant* element in finding love—traditionally, this wasn't the case.

- What you write in your profile and e-mails makes an impression—*make a good first impression.*

- You can determine important nuances of someone's personality by *what and how that person communicates.*

- *Most people are honest,* but for sure there are people online that are not always telling the truth.

Chapter 11

Filling in the White Spaces
A Variety of Informational Nuggets That Further Describe How Online Dating Can Work for You

I observed many other things while online. Many of these topics are bite-size morsels of information. Oftentimes, the beauty of a picture on a canvas is not just in the broad strokes but also in the short strokes, the finer points. The integration of both broad and short strokes creates your masterpiece. I have covered the market for online dating, profile creation, and contact management. These are big foundational elements in this space. We are now going to speed-date through a number of topics to bring you more nuances of the online dating experience.

The Hunted Become the Hunters

Online dating has changed the traditional male and female roles. Men were typically the hunters, and women were typically the hunted. Before the Internet, I had to read a woman's signals (e.g., her smile or lack thereof) to determine whether she was interested in me before I made my advance toward her. Sometimes I read her correctly, and I was successful. Other times, when I wasn't getting a clear signal and misread things, I was not so successful. Guys gambled all the time on whether the woman would respond to their advances. The dating scene can seem as unpredictable as a lion chasing a gazelle across the Serengeti. Sometimes it eats, and sometimes it doesn't. We don't need any pity over this. It is just the way that it is. That is the price of being the hunter.

I am sure that there have many times when a woman was interested in me but I was being a little thick in the head and wasn't picking up on the signals from her. It wouldn't be the first time that I was being a little Forrest Gump about things, well intentioned but slow. The point is that you sometimes really don't know who is interested in you. The Internet, for some reason, liberates women to initiate contact and approach others with much more confidence than they would ever display in person. Their gestures are unambiguous. Guys have a clear idea who is interested.

Online, women are much more courageous and forthright about who they are and what they desire in a relationship. As a man, I liked this unsolicited attention. In general, there is more emotional safety online when initiating a contact. This makes the sting of rejection less severe, which probably makes it easier for women to step out there.

Men are not playing the hunter role as extensively as they once did. Women are licking their chops just the same. Most women still like to be pursued, but online dating has empowered them with another option. This cultural shift will play a prominent role in your online dating experience.

Is It Difficult to Pick Someone from Your Four-Person Rotation?

Online dating is a process of generating contacts and receiving unsolicited contacts from new people. Sure, I learned that it was more prudent not to have more than four people in the rotation. The question that kept arising was, how do I choose which person to move forward with? Most of the ladies in my four-spot rotation were nice. Again, it was great to have so many options to consider. Sometimes I found it a little challenging to finally settle on one person. If one or all of the four didn't work out, there was always another seemingly great woman who was just waiting for me to send an e-mail.

I talked to a female friend of mine who had decided to begin looking for a man online. Without any guiding or prodding, she expressed the same kind of confusion. She told me sort of sheepishly, "This online thing is going pretty good, but sometimes it can be hard to decide who to pick." It was a relief to hear her say this, because I then realized that it wasn't just me, and neither was it just a male thing.

I don't think that you can attribute this to a fickle condition of youth either. As for me, I dated online during my early to mid-thirties and was intent on finding a significant relationship. My friend is now in her late thirties. She wants to be married and have children, but with the unprecedented array of options before her, she has struggled to choose.

For me, the prospect of waiting for another unsolicited e-mail or the prospect of finding someone new by conducting my own search always held out the potential for someone fresh who was even more promising than the four in my rotation. Each new person represents a potential pot at the end of the rainbow.

Stop Chasing Rainbows

Is online dating just like chasing a rainbow? Rainbows captivated us as children. I remember how, on summer afternoons just after a midday shower, the sun would emerge from the clouds and the whole neighborhood would be graced with a beautiful rainbow. As kids, we were always fascinated by the brilliance of rainbows and how they just appeared out of nowhere, sort of like that beautiful new person who just sent you an e-mail.

During a time when I was not quite a teenager, a rainbow appeared after a shower. My friends and I screamed, "Look at the rainbow!" We oohed and ahed at it, and then we got on our bikes and tried to chase the sky until we found the end of the rainbow. We rode on our bikes for blocks and blocks. It felt like miles and miles. We never did find the end of that rainbow. We finally gave up in exhaustion, but we were so glad for the chase. After all those years and chases, we never found the promised pot at the end of the rainbow.

Is online dating deceptive that way? Does it draw you in with the beauty of its colors? Do the great smiles, personalities, and cultural sensibilities do it for you? Does the next great profile or set of pictures do just enough to cause you to wonder what the new people are like? This deceptive allure can entangle both men and women. If you are not aware, you can get on that treadmill, chasing that rainbow, that man or woman of your dreams. Many people looking for love online face this reality. The constant allure of a chase for something better is what helps to solidify the realities of the *two* in the two-by-four rule. The constant stimulation keeps you primed for the next great guy or lady. It fuels the turnover online. People are frequently looking for something better.

Keeping this treadmill mentality will keep you from finding your best match. Don't be duped by it. There is no need to panic or be apprehensive because of the increased number of choices that you may have. Just know that this dynamic is what you will encounter online in a way that you typically don't experience in your daily physical life.

My advice to you is this: (1) don't be afraid of the increased number of choices, and (2) don't be afraid to choose one person. You have to be clear with yourself about what you want. When you find the person, make the decision to move forward. Remember that even people who are perfect for each other have shortcomings and personality quirks. Rainbows are nice, but they are usually temporary. Don't let the chase be your goal; let the chase lead you to your goal.

Choosing Profiles with or without Photos

Photos—how important are they? I touched on this earlier in the book but wanted to spend a little additional time with it. No matter which dating service you select, you are going to choose profiles with or without photos and potentially both. Which is better? Love is like art: it is in the eye of the beholder. I would say that it depends. Certainly, if you decide to select profiles both with and without photos, you materially increase the number of people you can sift through.

Selecting profiles without photos puts you in a position where you have to be very discerning. You will be missing an important element in determining whether to contact someone. I usually skewed much more toward profiles with photos. The Internet hasn't changed people. Looks do matter. We still make our judgments about people with some serious consideration about how they physically look. Physical attraction is an important element in forming one person's overall attraction for another. It may take only a cute smile, a nice hairstyle, or a trim waistline. Whatever floats your boat is up to you, but we have to be honest with ourselves that it is a part of our consideration process. Even if someone's looks are not a material consideration, at least that person would like to know what he or she is getting into.

The Use of Video

Since 1999, the Internet has changed dramatically. How people are willing to use it has changed as well. Initially there was no video capability to enhance the online dating experience. This changed a few years into it. Now, video is everywhere on the Net. You can watch some serious news on one of the major news sites or view some goofy thirty-second clip on Youtube.com. Video is a great little feature. Some dating sites allow you to post video clips as an introduction for prospective viewers. This is a nice teaser.

I did use video when conducting IM conversations. Adding video substantially enhanced the depth and quality of the interaction. I would make contact with a woman, or she would contact me, and we would decide to go into an IM session with video. Such conversations are similar to meeting someone at a friend's dinner party; actually, they are better than a dinner party. You get the benefit of prescreening the person by viewing his or her profile before starting your IM session. Sometimes this can be a better starting place than a typical first-time in-person connection. The trade-off is that usually neither of you is dressed very nice. I was usually in some shorts and a T-shirt. The woman usually was not looking her best either.

Adding video just makes the experience much better. I give the use of video high marks.

Are You Guilty of Revealing Too Much Information (TMI) Online?

Occasionally someone in a group of people will share information that is too revealing. The information is a little embarrassing to hear, because you don't know the person who is speaking very well. We are all familiar with these experiences.

A group of friends and distant acquaintances have dinner. There is a good conversation going when suddenly, after someone is asked to pass the bread, one of the distant acquaintances shares information about how he once suffered from food poisoning. The story would have been fine, but he proceeded to talk about the details of how he couldn't leave the bathroom. He goes on and on. People's noses begin to turn up at the imagery in their minds as they try to eat their salads. You have to interject and say, "Okay, enough already. That is just too much information [TMI] for me to know!"

Some people can be that way online. I love the fact that people are much more revealing about who they are during conversations. The benefit is that you can get to know a large amount of personal information about the person in a short period of time. You can quickly cover the topics of your career, siblings, likes, and dislikes. I love that aspect. As with most things, moderation is the operative word.

There were several instances when I would be twenty to thirty minutes into the conversation and the woman would start to share how her previous boyfriend had cheated on her badly and that she was still sad about this and hoped that it wouldn't happen again. I was sympathetic and really didn't have plans to behave like her previous boyfriends, but I thought, "Wow, this is some heavy information and probably shouldn't be shared within the first twenty minutes of meeting someone." This sort of thing would happen all the time.

You can't control what people say and when they say it, so I learned to go with the flow. I always thought that it was a turnoff, because it was an indication that this person had not gotten over the previous experience, which meant that she was not ready for me. Online dating creates a dynamic of openness, but don't lose your TMI sensor. Moderation and timing are key here.

Playing Ignorant—Why Do We Do It?

Why do people sometimes play ignorant when they send you an unsolicited e-mail? Why? On the surface, finding a mate online seems to be one of the most cut-and-dried things you can do. You are effectively preordering the group of people who match the criteria that you are looking for. It is almost like going to Burger King. You can have it your way, onions or no onions—you decide.

Placing a query is somewhat similar. A woman can pick a man who lives two towns over, works as an engineer, likes to hike, and sits in cafes and reads the *New York Times* on Sunday afternoons. This is equally true for men. A guy can spell out in his search criteria that he has a preference for brunettes, a woman who weighs between 120 and 150 pounds, someone who loves dogs, and so on.

Just as people are specific in their searches, they are also specific in their profiles about the kind of person they desire. Oftentimes, people sending unsolicited e-mails do not respect the specificity of the criteria identified in the profile. No one is going to match your desired mate 100 percent, but the unsolicited e-mail should at least be close.

People will pretend to be ignorant of the criteria laid out in the profile of their desired match. Before the e-mail is sent out, they know that their profile is not a good match for the other person's. They won't be deterred, because their heart is racing. Because their emotions are palpable, they play ignorant regarding the material mismatch in personality and wants. The guy hopes that this new lady will see him as he sees her: as a perfect match. She just needs to respond to his e-mail.

The Words of a Woman Who Was E-X-A-S-P-E-R-A-T-E-D

I have read more than a few profiles of women who have stated emphatically in their profiles, "I will not respond to e-mails from guys who live more than twenty-five miles away!" You get the sense that long-distance relationships are not their thing. Some women write in their profiles, "I will not respond to messages without photos!" It is as if these people are screaming, "Read and comply with the profile before you send me a message please!" She was obviously tired of the headless profiles jamming her in-box. You could almost feel the fury in each typed word. These are the words of women who were just fed up with people playing ignorant.

She Tried to Pull a Fast One—Men Are Not the Only Ones Guilty of Playing Ignorant

I remember on one Saturday evening, I was online, as I had been so many other evenings, pounding away at the keyboard, clicking profiles, and typing e-mails. All of a sudden, I got a message from a woman from Italy, and she wanted to have an IM conversation. I did the customary profile review of her before I accepted, and after taking a look, I thought, "Awesome! I just hit the jackpot!" This woman was gorgeous, and she met a lot of my criteria.

We commenced an IM conversation, and things were going swimmingly for about thirty minutes. I was dreaming of my next trip to Italy. I imagined myself sipping espressos, eating gelato while strolling in the piazzas, and enjoying the frenetic Italian conversations, when somehow the topic of what I was going to do the next day came up. Of course I told her what I was going to do—go to church.

I naturally asked her what she was doing the next day. This was when it became apparent that she was playing ignorant. She decided to try and negotiate around her answer. It turned out that her avoidance was a red flag that I couldn't ignore. Well, I soon discovered that she was an atheist. I immediately thought, "What in the world were you thinking? You had to have read my profile. You decided to send me an e-mail first." I had not only checked the box on my profile indicating that I am a Christian but also mentioned in the text of my description that this was an important area in my life.

What we had here was a square peg trying to go into a round hole. In an instant, the dream of espressos and gelato was dashed on the shores of reality. Like other mismatches, I had to toss her back. Such is the way of online dating.

At times I have been guilty of the same crime. My emotions had gotten the best of me. I had created false hope. Unfortunately, this kind of willful disregard for truth doesn't fulfill hopes but causes an annoyance. Imagine receiving five or more of these mismatched messages a week. It would get old quick. You can't make someone like you if you are not their type. My advice is to avoid playing ignorant. It is a waste of everyone's time.

Are People Online More or Less Sane?

I was in a bar one night recently, listening to a friend's band. I met some of his friends, and we talked about dating online. One of the women said that she wouldn't try online dating because the people that you meet online are "crazy" and that all of her friends told her the same about people online. I am sure that there are many people who feel similarly. Online dating is still relatively new. It represents the unknown, and that makes some people feel uncomfortable and probably a little fearful.

When I first began meeting women online in 1999, there may have been a higher percentage of desperate people online, because they were willing to engage in an activity that was commonly referred to as "weird." However, being desperate doesn't make you "crazy." Most people who date online are just as stable as anyone else. Absolutely, there are people online that are off their rockers. However, it would be paranoid to think that everyone is that way. What is funny is that somehow people act as if they never realized that some people were a little off their rockers before online dating.

My Encounter with Someone Who Was Momentarily Unstable

Sure, I have run across people online who were off their rockers. I included an example of one of my experiences. It would be disingenuous of me to overemphasize the positives and not present a balanced view.

I met a woman once on one of the mainline sites. She had an amazing personality. She was so full of energy and was incredibly positive, but one of the things that bothered me from the outset was that she was just a party animal. When she wasn't partying, she was great. She would party two or three nights during the workweek. That is heavy partying. Every time that we talked, she would tell me how she and her girlfriend would party until 4 AM. I was always floored by the idea of dancing until that hour of the morning, particularly if I had to go to work the next day. Even in my intense partying days, I never went much later than 2 AM, so when she told me that she partied a couple of times a week until 4 AM, I knew that I could not keep up with her pace; I wasn't sure if we would make it very far. My intuition was spot-on but for this and other reasons.

Outside of the partying, we had very good conversations. I was definitely starting to like her, and it was clear that her feelings were even stronger for me. After about five weeks, she expressed very direct thoughts about how she felt about me. She made it clear that she thought that we could be married and have a great life together. I told her that I was not afraid to move quickly but not that quickly. I really did like her, but five weeks was too soon for me to be considering marriage with her.

She would not be deterred. Every other day, she would persist in pressuring me to consider marrying her. I had to be clear with her every time that we didn't need to rush. She was just so unrelenting. She took what I thought was responsible expectation setting as complete rejection. This naturally began to make for strained conversations. She soon began to get overly emotional in our discussions by hanging up the phone abruptly several times. A quick apology would always follow. This erratic behavior sounded the alarm that this woman had some problems with her emotions on a number of fronts

I soon discovered this in a more profound way. By this time, we were just over six weeks into the relationship. I was starting to get an uncomfortable feeling about this woman. I thought that it would be best to bring things to an end. I wasn't up for this kind of grilling and erratic behavior, particularly since were just getting started with our connection. If we had been together for a year or so, I would have tried to search for a different solution.

My statement that we had to end things really flipped her switch. After that difficult conversation, there were follow-up discussions that had the customary back-and-forth about how we should be together. Remember, it had been only six weeks. Once she realized that I would not be persuaded, she had a complete meltdown. By the following day, I received seventeen desperate and harassing phone calls. I took the first few calls, but then I realized that I couldn't continue to enable her antics. I had to stop answering the phone. She left more than fourteen messages overnight.

Most of the messages were tear-filled about how life was over for her. She threatened to commit suicide. In fact, her good friend even called me the next day, expressing how concerned she was for her friend's welfare. I was thinking, "Dang, it can't be all that serious. It was only six weeks!" She had also decided to quit her job and move near me so that we could be together.

Needless to say, I was a little freaked out by the unexpected breakdown. Fortunately, the next day, I was able to reason with her about the value of life. I thank God that there was no suicide. She did actually quit her job. I thought that she didn't need to mess up things in her life over our six-week relationship, so I told her firmly that she needed to go back to work to attempt to resecure her job. I think that it was what she needed, because she promptly went to work the next day to get her job back. The relationship, as you might expect, was over. We both went back to cyberspace to search for the right mate.

Are people more or less sane online? The question should be, Are people, in general, more or less sane? You will find extreme behaviors everywhere. Don't throw out the baby with the bathwater. The benefits of online dating far exceed the potential negatives from these very infrequent occurrences.

What to Consider If You Meet Someone from a Foreign Country

The topic of international dating presents unique dynamics that warrant a little extra time. You are almost guaranteed to meet someone from a different country. There are literally millions of single people around the world who are trying to find love using online dating sites. They may be looking for you, and you may be looking for them. Because you are destined to meet someone from abroad, is there something in particular that you need to consider?

The answer is no and yes. The reason I say no is that people are fundamentally the same. Women in the United States want happiness in their relationships, as do women from the UK, Mexico, and Japan. The same holds true for men. How one articulates happiness may be slightly different due to personality and cultural uniqueness, but the fundamentals of it are the same. Don't be intimidated by the differences. They provide a fantastic opportunity for you to grow and learn together.

Here is the yes portion of the answer. There are some things that you will come across once you meet someone from abroad. This is a short list of substantive items that will familiarize you with international encounters.

Language Differences—Sharing a common language is one of those essentials for fruitful communication. Many people who are citizens of countries outside the United States speak English as a second or third language. Consequently, they have more options as to the number of people with whom they can contact, which means that people in the United States are likely to receive a message from someone from another country. It was very common for me to receive messages from women from the UK, Germany, Spain, Mexico, Italy, and others. Because I didn't speak another language, the proficiency of that person's English is what determined the quality of our communications. A slight accent is cute. Even someone speaking without a complete command of English can also be cute, though slightly less so. However, if the person struggles to communicate their thoughts in relatively cogent sentences, then things cease being cute.

In fact, if the dialogue is too cryptic, it can lead to frustration. If you have important things in common with someone and the language differences make communications tough but not impossible, work at it. You may have found the love of your life. If you can't understand anything beyond "Hi" and "I am fine," unfortunately it will be best that you toss the person back to cyberspace.

This happened to me with a lovely lady from Brazil. Her English proficiency was bad. My Portuguese proficiency was infinitely worse than her English. It was unrealistic to think that either of us would learn the other's language before we tired of the situation.

Geographical Distance—Most people who speak a foreign language as their primary language but also speak English live a long distance from the United States. Mexico and the French-speaking portion of Canada are the two areas that are the closest. Most other places are an overnight flight away.

This means you will have substantially fewer opportunities for in-person interactions. This is not the end of all possibilities. E-mails and phone conversations will be the main way that you develop your relationship. You can certainly enhance your experience by utilizing video either through IM functionality or through Internet phone service providers such as Skype. If things get serious, you will want to see each other. This isn't the worst thing in the world. At least now you have a reason to update your passport.

Cultural Nuances—People are the same, but they tend to do things just a little differently. These nuances can modify your expectations for a relationship. Italians use the term *fiancé* as way to identify a serious dating relationship. It is not used as a way to identify someone's soon-to-be spouse, as it is used in the United States.

Political and social views could also be materially different. The United States is the closest that the world has to a modern-day Roman

Empire. The United States comes into contact with and influences a lot of countries. Some of those encounters are perceived positively, whereas others are not. As a result, some people that you meet from other countries may have different perspectives about America than you have. Some of them may possess slightly negative or cynical views. Many people are very quick to hold a mirror up to help Americans see how the United States impacts the world, particularly for much smaller and less influential countries.

I took a lot of grief for President George W. Bush. If the person disagrees with the policies of the United States, you may be asked to specify where you stand on certain topics. This was a common occurrence for me. In the United States, the conflict might be red states versus blue states, but with international online dating, it is American political policies versus global sentiment.

There will be many other nuances beyond the two specified here. Keep an open mind, and stay respectful when this conversation comes along. You'll learn about different customs and mind-sets. If these differences present too large an obstacle, then maybe you should move on. You are not trying to conduct foreign diplomacy. You are trying to find a mate.

Patience—When dealing with something new and a bit unknown, exercising patience is a good approach. It is very possible to meet a great person who lives in another country. You just have to approach the situation with the same seriousness that you apply to potential relationships with people from your home country. You'll certainly have a few miscues but nothing that should prevent you from being open to the prospect of an international match.

"I Am Somebody!" ... and So Are They—Treat People with Respect

It was 1988. Jesse Jackson was giving Michael Dukakis a serious run for the Democratic presidential nomination. It was an intense race that came down to the wire. All of that effort didn't lead either man to his intended goal, the office of the president of the United States.

The first George Bush who ran for president would prove to be victorious, and he became this nation's forty-first president. There are two things that I will never forget about that Democratic primary race: (1) Willie Horton, who ultimately "did in" Michael Dukakis's race for the White House, and (2) Jesse Jackson's celebrated impassioned plea to Americans to proclaim, "I am somebody!"

René Descartes stated, "I think; therefore I am," which may seem a little obvious, but Jesse Jackson recognized that there was tremendous power in a people awakening to a reality regarding their humanity.

What do the events of 1988 have to do with online dating? Jesse Jackson based his platform on the value of people's humanity. It struck a chord. You will meet a lot of people while dating online. They will be real people with real feelings and real lives. Remember the humanity of man—yours and theirs. It might become easy to forget with the turnover of potential contacts. Don't let the pace of the process cause you to overlook other people's humanity. Be honest and kind in your interactions. Treat people as you would want them to treat you. You may figuratively toss people back or be tossed back, but make every effort to be kind along the way. Don't forget one thing. Jesse said it best: "I am somebody!" And I'm saying to you, "So are they."

Stop Dating and Start Courting

Next to the two-by-four rule, this is one of the more important techniques in the book. After all the dating that has occurred, it is clear that a different approach is in order. People have been dating too long, and it has caused all sorts of disappointments. People largely struggle to find the person that is right for them. They dig themselves out of one bad long-term relationship after another. All the while, they invest significant time in a process that has not given them the relationship that they were hoping for.

What Is Dating?

This is what most people do when they meet someone new. They exchange numbers. It doesn't matter where you meet the person. You talk on the phone a bit, which usually leads to some in-person activity. It could be anything—dinner, lunch, coffee, or just a walk. Many times, unless they find out that your name is Oil and you find out that his name is Water, there is a high likelihood that you will meet again.

Now You Are Just Hanging Out

Things are going really well with this person. You are very glad to see the person again and again. In between these dates, there are a number of conversations on the phone that help to transition you between activities. This rhythm of chatting and outings, if all goes well, will usually progress for several months, which will include holidays and birthdays. This can go on for possibly a year or more. At this point, both of you really have a strong sense for the other person. This intimacy level will steadily increase.

As time goes by, there are usually no expectations or ideas for where things may go, because people are usually just hanging out. There may or may not have been a discussion about whether you are dating exclusively. It is possible that exclusivity in the relationship isn't discussed explicitly. This wouldn't be uncommon. Again, people are usually just hanging out. However, just hanging out significantly reduces the chances of you discovering whether this person is a right fit for you.

Things That You Never Discussed That Later Become a Problem

How many times have we heard stories about relationships that were seriously struggling or had failed after one person realized that the other person was not on the same page with him or her about something important? For example, one person can resolve conflict only through screaming or violence. Unfortunately, after a year or two of this, the other person realizes that they can't take it anymore. Or how many people discover late into the relationship that their partner doesn't believe in the institution of marriage and doesn't want to be constrained in this way? You, on the other hand, know that this has been one of your lifelong dreams. You can miss all kinds of things that can derail your love train, particularly when you are just hanging out.

Traditional Dating Isn't a Disaster, but There Is a Better Way

I don't want to criticize traditional dating too strongly. We know that this approach does work for some people. Every year, between May and September, the reception halls around America are booked every weekend, churning out newly minted married couples as quickly as GM churns out automobiles. Then again, we also know that there are many people who never translate the years invested in traditional dating to marriage. Courting is the better way. Courting will move you substantially closer to finding the right person.

What Is Courting?

Like traditional dating, courting is a way for people to get to know each other in a dating relationship. Courting is, however, different. This is a notion that might appear to be a throwback concept from a generation or two ago. There is a reason why it works. Here are two main differences when considering courting relative to traditional dating.

1. **Mind-set difference**—*Change the purpose in your mind for why you are spending time with this person.* Courting starts out with an underlying objective of finding out whether this is someone with whom you can establish at least a meaningful and committed relationship. Marriage isn't always the primary goal, but if done right, courting can put you in a better spot to consider this as an option. Courting relies on a mind-set that is very different from what you might see in someone who is dating in the traditional sense. The casual attitude of "We'll see how and where it goes" is not the leading thought, and it is not even on your mind.

2. Dialogue difference—*Change the nature of your dialogue when try-ing to create a relationship*. You have to be purposeful in your conversa-tions. You want to find out whether this person shares your position on things that are important. You should be much more probative in your discussions. Your questions should be specific. For example, questions like "Do you want children?" "Is marriage important to you?" and "Where do you stand on matters of faith?" are questions that should be posed. Don't ask these questions in rapid-fire succes-sion. It shouldn't feel like the Spanish Inquisition. There should be plenty of time for idle chitchat as well as going out for dinner and to the movies.

Therein lies the most important dialogue difference. If someone doesn't meet your important criteria and there is no room for com-promise, you have to tell that person that you are not compatible and move forward without him or her. You should be able to make this determination much sooner than would be possible with traditional dating. This should probably happen before you get two years into it.

Being Clear Will Serve You Best

Courting is respectful but clear. The benefits of being clear are as fol-lows: (1) you are honest with the other person about what is impor-tant to you, (2) you set expectations and boundaries that are essential for a relationship to succeed, and (3) you don't waste your precious time in a relationship that you know can't be salvaged.

Approaching dating under the guise of courting should help you get more out of your relationships. It will help you separate the meat from the fat or separate the wheat from the chaff—you pick the metaphor.

A Recap Before We Pull Up Anchor

- Women are *increasingly the hunters* in online dating.

- Don't let the chase be your goal. *Use the chase* to help you reach your goal.

- Picking profiles with photos *reduces the ambiguity* that might be more common with profiles without photos.

- *Video is great enhancer* to IM conversations.

- Sometimes people share *too much information (TMI)* early in the contact. Sharing is good but in moderation.

- Sometimes people *play ignorant* regarding the criteria in your profile.

- Generally, *people online are of a sound mind*, though there are always exceptions.

- *International contacts—four things to consider:* (1) language differences, (2) geographic distance, (3) cultural nuances, and (4) patience.

- Treat *people* with respect.

- Stop dating and start *courting*.

Chapter 1 2

The Great Stumbling Block

I was over five years into dating online, and I hadn't found that pot of gold at the end of the rainbow. I felt as though I was on a fairly bad streak.

I was certainly meeting a wide range and sufficient number of women online, but I was not having success in taking one of those relationships to the next level. There was one issue in particular that presented itself as a consistent stumbling block. It ultimately led me to shut down five relationships in a row. Either I was incredibly effective at tossing back contacts that were not right for me or I was consistently making mistakes. I couldn't quite tell, but I wasn't feeling great about it. I was thinking, "What happened to the Internet being such a great place to meet the love of your life?" You just have to put in your criteria and order them up, right?

There Was Always a Day of Reckoning

This is how it would go. There would be an initial connection, either from me or from the woman. She would be intriguing, and we would get along great. We would sail right past the *two* in the two-by-four rule. We would meet, and things would be generally very positive. Then, naturally, we would move progressively to even more substantive discussions. The first indication that there might be a problem would always arise when I would describe what I did during the day. Ordinarily, this would not be a cause for concern. However, Sunday would always be the day of reckoning. I would talk about having gone to church that morning. Then I would elaborate on what had happened at lunch with some friends from church. It was fairly straightforward.

However, there was often an awkwardness that followed that began to reveal the hidden crack in the supposedly stable foundation of our developing relationship. It would become clear that we were not on the same page about something very important, our faith. The crack always existed. We were just now discovering it. You might ask, "Well, if you made it past the *two* in the two-by-four rule, how is it that a discussion about church presented a potential problem?" Well, as you know, it takes time to get to know people, even when you are courting.

The women had checked the box that indicated that they were Christian, so I felt that we were on safe ground. Also, it is not very typical to start a contact with someone new by saying, "Hi. I'm Myles. I liked your profile. I see that you are a Christian. What do you think about Isaiah, chapter 53?" Nobody talks like that, and certainly such talk would scare just about anyone away. However, from then on, my warning sensors would continually let me know that there was a problem. It was sort of like the engine light on your car dash: you can ignore it, but the problem is not going away, and you need to address it.

What People Checked Wasn't Always What I Got

My general tack was to let the topic pass on by and to continue to get to know them. I had it in my mind to revisit the subject of faith in the future. Eventually, I would decide to discuss the topic more directly.

During these discussions, I would find myself going back and forth with these women about a variety of topics concerning faith. The discussions ranged from dual-faith households and atheism versus belief in God to the possibility of not believing in Jesus while still being a Christian. All of these discussions were had with women who had indicated that they were followers of Jesus Christ. The unfortunate result was that none of these conversations led to a uniting of mind-sets.

In the context of dating, people are not likely to change. They are who they are. They usually don't change their minds on important issues during dating. If someone is adamantly against the institution of marriage, he or she is unlikely to be persuaded to think otherwise during the course of your relationship. This was the case for me with regard to faith in God. I wanted my relationship with Jesus to affect my choice in mate, but some of the women that I met didn't feel similarly or at least were not sure. Dating relationships are not the place to make someone a new person.

These experiences confirmed one thing that I had known. You can't try to change people. These experiences also taught me one thing: even though it seems highly reasonable to regard the contents of people's profiles as accurate, sometimes what people check on their profile isn't always what you get.

I Had the Right Approach, but I Forgot One Very Important Thing

The issue was why I had, knowingly or not, decided to go it alone in the search for a mate. As you can probably gather, I am a believer in Jesus Christ. That means that I believe that Jesus is the Son of God and that he died for the redemption of man's soul for those that would believe in him. I believe this by faith. Because of this, I have eternal life with God when my life is over. God is always with me. He knows everything about me. He knows my wants and my needs.

Even with God Almighty available to meet all my needs, I did as most people do. I had forgotten God in the midst of my situation. Christians and non-Christians are all prone to adopt this go-it-alone mind-set. I hadn't asked Him one time to intervene and meet my need for a wife. I didn't ask Him one time to change me so that I would be ready to be a good partner for a potential mate.

As I confronted repeated disappointments, I discovered that my relationship with Christ was more than an accessory to my life that I put on every Sunday. He was and is integrated into my consciousness, shaping every aspect of my life. After I had that epiphany, I began to pray for God to provide a woman for me and to make me ready for that person. I knew that God would be faithful and answer my prayer.

My life has continually been taken to new levels of joy and contentment since coming to faith in Jesus. If you are a Christian, I encourage you not to forget God in the midst of your need. If you are not a Christian, I can understand it if you are thinking, "Well, I am not a Christian, so I guess you aren't talking to me." This message is for you too. Regardless of where you are spiritually, I would be remiss if I didn't invite you to consider the claims of Christianity. The peace and freedom of Christ is available to all those who have yet to come to accept Him.

Not only do your prospects of finding a spouse go up with God, but also the certainly of a new life is set before you. It is much easier than you think. When I came to believe in Jesus, I recognized that how I led my life and how I thought had completely fallen short of His glory and holiness. But I knew that I wanted the wholeness that is available through Him. I just acknowledged in my heart that Jesus is the Son of God who died for my sins, that I had sinned and had fallen short of God's glory, and that by faith I wanted and accepted Him as the Lord of my life. I joined a bible-based church and I have never been the same since that time. It was not a secret waiting to be discovered. It was about the person of Jesus. It was that simple. From that point on, God has been with me, giving me a new purpose in life. I know that I can take all of my cares to Him. Though I had momentarily forgotten, this also included my desires for a spouse. Because of my belief in Jesus, I am considered righteous in the eyes of God and God hears the prayers of the righteous.

So this is what I had forgotten. I had forgotten God and prayer. All of the techniques were still important. I still had to use my judgment to discern whether someone would be the right person for me. I still had to manage the contacts. It was just important for me to remember that I shouldn't try to live my life alone. I recommend that neither should you.

Just Keep Looking

So this is how it went. This cycle would happen again and again. Some of the relationships lasted two months and one as long as six months. I knew that there had to be some sort of solution out there. The Internet has almost no limits in terms of the subjects that are available to be searched. I just needed to think a bit harder in order to exploit this "have it your way" medium.

So, because finding someone who was Christian was becoming a really important quality to look for in a mate, I wanted to have a keener eye for this when I met the next woman. I went back to the search engines, looking for Web sites that specialized in Christian dating. As you might have expected, there were several sites: Christian Singles, ChristianCafe.com, and so on. Most of the mainline sites also had Web pages dedicated to my particular desire for Christians. I eventually chose to go with ChristianCafe.com, which turned out to be just what I was looking for.

A Recap Before We Pull Up Anchor

- *What you see is what you get* with people.

- When dating, don't try to change another person's *deeply held beliefs*.

- Don't try to live your life alone—*keep God in the midst of your situation*.

- If you haven't found the right person, *just keep looking*.

Chapter 13

The Wink That Changed My Life Forever

I signed up for ChristianCafe.com because they had a larger membership base than the other Christian sites. Even with this advantage, it was definitely a specialty online dating site. There were far fewer total members on this site relative to the mainline sites. I didn't feel that this was going to be a problem. I was hoping that the targeted nature of this site would help address my dating challenge.

The Sun Quietly Sets on the Summer

Nothing too eventful happened in my dating life during the summer of 2005. I had been on the site for just about a couple of months. I had joined during the summer, so I was out of the house or out of town most of that time. Most other people are active during the summer and out of the house as well. Even with the active summer, I was identifying a relatively decent number of potential contacts. I was also getting a reasonable number of unsolicited messages.

I had some interesting conversations with women from various places. I met one woman that showed some real promise. The problem was that she was a professional singer and traveled the world regularly for different performances. We really wanted to meet, but it never happened. As a result, we both lost interest and tossed each other back. There were a few other contacts that nearly budded into something meaningful. However, none of them could make it past the two-week mark. The summer came to an end. There was no new lady in my life, but I was still optimistic about things.

The Coincidence That Triggered Curiosity

It was early September. I was gearing up for the fall, when I noticed the profile of a woman. There was a photo of her in the cockpit of a helicopter. She looked as though she was having fun, and the landscape appeared to be somewhere outside of the United States. The wind had blown her hair mildly across her face. It looked as though the mid-afternoon sun had caused a slight shadow to be cast over her face, but her smile still peered through. The photo suggested that she was a woman of joy and contentment, but it also revealed a sense of adventure. I was intrigued by it. What really caught my eye was her birthday, April 21. It is the same birthday as mine!

She was two years younger than I, but I had never met another woman whose birthday was the same as mine. Was this a sign? I wasn't exactly sure, but I knew that we automatically had something in common. I was also immediately aware that we were a little different. First of all, she was Norwegian. Second, she was living in Oslo, Norway. I was, on the other hand, living in New Jersey in the United States. I wasn't daunted. Of course, with our common birthday presenting such a provocative invitation, how could I not satisfy my curiosity? So, I "winked" at her, hoping she would reply—and then who knew what might happen? A wink, by the way, is a button found on the user interface of most online dating sites that essentially allows you to tap the person on the shoulder and say, "*Psst* ... hey ... I think that you are kind of cute and interesting. You want to chat?" It is harmless and requires very little effort or creativity.

Who Was This Lady?

It was starting to look as though this site was going to pay dividends for me. She winked back at me, letting me know that she was interested. So we were on our way.

I like to travel. Europe has always been one of my favorite places. Norway, however, was not on my short list of countries to visit. It is a very small country with only 4.5 million people. I didn't know much about the country or the people. I soon discovered that they are a welcoming and open people. The French may like their cheeses and the Italians may love their pasta, but the Norwegians love their bread. It also gets very cold there. A portion of it touches the northern part of Russia.

The infamous Vikings originated from Scandinavia, which included Norway. Physically, I could imagine her as a Viking. She had thick and long hair to protect her from the blistering Scandinavian winters. She also had deep blue eyes to help her survive the lack of sun in the northern latitude.

It turned out that this Viking had never been as daring in her dating life as I had been. At that point in time, I had logged more than five years of e-mailing, clicking, winking, and IMing in the pursuit of a meaningful relationship. She, on the other hand, had begun her maiden voyage with Internet dating just two weeks prior to our connection. She was a late adopter.

Was There Serendipity in Norway?

She had been out of a relationship for about three years and was interested in finding someone new. What was ironic was that the only reason that she was even considering online dating was that she had to reduce the busyness of her life. Two weeks prior to our connection, she had fallen from her bike and broken her left arm. This injury prevented her from performing her duties at work. She was working as a midwife. As you know, midwives deliver babies, so they need to have both arms functioning and strong to assist women in bringing new life into the world.

Because her arm was immobile, she was at home doing nothing but trying to mend herself. She considered giving online dating a try because she had so much free time on her hands. She began by putting a profile online at a site that she thought would be the correct match for her dating preferences. ChristianCafe.com was it for her. Two weeks later, there I was knocking on her virtual door.

If it hadn't been for her unfortunate mishap with her bike and our common birth dates, we probably would have never met. What should I make of this? Was it serendipity or divine conspiracy? The one thing that I was sure of was that there was a great chance here for something meaningful.

The Two-Week Mark in My Rearview Mirror

Straight off, we connected. It turned out that the photo of her was taken while she was flying over an African landscape. I thought that this was a good sign, because I like to travel and explore new places whenever possible. Remember what I said about how you can determine things from the photo that someone places online? We went through the customary information exchange in the e-mails that we sent. She was very pleasant in our communications. As she told me about her life over the weeks that followed, it was becoming clearer that I was really growing fond of her. She was gentle but strong and independent. Even with all of my experience in dating online, meeting people from across America and across the globe, I would never have guessed that I would meet someone from Norway.

As we were sailing smoothly beyond the two in the two-by-four rule, I was pleasantly surprised by how willingly she began telling me about her Sunday activities, which included her afternoons at church. I thought, "Finally." I didn't even have to direct the conversation. Her initiation made for very smooth conversations as we talked about the totality of our weeks. It was beginning to feel like a match made in heaven. Well, I was encouraged, but I also knew that common faith does not guarantee a happy relationship. I don't need to tell you about the striking and unfortunate similarity between the divorce rates of those who identify themselves as Christian and those who don't.

Because I had learned that I would be better served by courting instead of traditional dating, I knew that it was time to really discover where we both stood on important matters. If we were not on the same page on certain things, it would not matter that we had the same birth date or went to the same high school or lived three streets from each other. I told her that I had really enjoyed my experience dating online and that I had met and dated several women over the past five or so years, but I explained that I was now looking for someone to create something more concrete. I wasn't just interested in dating for the sake of dating or just killing time.

I explained to her that I was definitely of the courting mind-set instead of the traditional dating mind-set. I wasn't sure what she was going to think. Maybe she wanted to progress a bit more slowly. She might have said, "Dude, pump your brakes. What's the rush?" Even though I was not in a rush, I was just trying to be more direct in our interactions. Of course, I first had to explain to her what I meant by "traditional dating" and "courting."

Courting Was Bearing Fruit

Because it takes two to tango, I was more than glad that she understood where I was coming from. She was similarly interested in courting instead of traditional dating. I was thrilled with this, because I had tried courting with a few women before Ms. Norway. Those efforts didn't go over so well. Not every woman is interested in the more deliberate approach to relationships that accompanies courting.

Because we were of the same mind, a comfortable series of conversations followed. Our e-mail messages were fun, because we had great chemistry and freely expressed humor in the communications between us. This was the first time that I knowingly courted a woman online.

Believe it or not, we were really developing a very rich sense of each other. People wonder whether it is possible to achieve such familiarity online. I can tell you that yes, it is possible.

Most people would agree that active, positive, and consistent communication is essential for a thriving relationship. You will not be able to establish and deepen emotional intimacy without it. We certainly had that. Moving ahead with my Norwegian lady required that we stay active in our conversations. She was 3,600 miles away, and there was the Atlantic Ocean between us as well. The e-mails, after several weeks, turned into phone conversations. We added active cell phone text messaging to the phone calls that we made. All of this further enhanced our level of connection.

So many things were flowing very naturally. It finally felt as though I had gotten the person that I was looking for. We shared many things in common: faith, sense of humor, communication styles, and perspectives on family and children. I loved how we seemed to complement each other. I was able to discover this in a much shorter period of time because our conversations were much more focused.

Courting didn't influence the type of people that we were, but it substantially improved our understanding about whether we were on the same page concerning this relationship. She was a midwife, and I was fascinated with the nature of this woman who brought life into the world. Her tender and generous spirit was the pied piper for my heart. All of this was happening even though we hadn't held hands, kissed, or held each other in an embrace.

It Was Time to Meet

So, all of this was going well because of the Internet. I knew that none of this would matter much if we didn't jell as well in person. Relationships thrive and last through daily, in-person interaction. It was time to see if the online magic would translate to our first face-to-face meeting. I had such a special feeling about her; I knew that if I had this same feeling for her after our initial meeting, I would ask her to marry me. I left for Norway on Christmas Day for a ten-day visit.

The entire trip was everything I'd hoped it would be. She was truly an angel for me. Over the next several months, there would be a few trips back and forth for each of us to meet our respective families. Things were moving more smoothly than I could have designed. There was nothing forced about it. I knew that this was right.

As I look back on it, it almost feels like a blur. Things moved so fast. I was used to being in relationships for two years or more. We were both in our mid- to late thirties and felt that we were grown-up enough to make our own decisions as rapidly as we desired. We decided to marry on a beautiful weekend during May in Norway several months after our first physical meeting on a cold day in Oslo. She was raised in Fredrikstad, Norway, and I was raised in Detroit, Michigan. We found each other and are now married. How likely is that? The Internet can really bridge worlds.

A New Wife, a New Life

I have absolutely no complaints about my online experience. In fact, I am thrilled with it. I am very happy with my new wife and my new life. I am also proud to share that my wife and I just celebrated the birth of our first child. Adjusting to fatherhood is quite a life-changing experience. You learn to be much more accommodating, which is why I am typing the last pages of this book with one hand and holding my ten-day-old son with the other. I can only describe it as a tremendous blessing.

A Recap Before We Pull Up Anchor

- Look for an online dating site that *appeals to your interests.*

- Courting does *bear fruit.*

- Online dating, if done correctly, will *change your life.*

Chapter 14

Dropping Anchor for the Last Time

Who would have imagined that something with a *.com* on the end of it could change my life so profoundly? I could not have. I had no great visionary expectations when I started more than six years ago.

For me, it was an exciting voyage on the seas of life. I used several online dating service providers while fishing for love on the Net. I fished in different ponds, hoping that each new online dating service provider would have in its member base the woman that had motivated my pursuit, my true love. A lot of potential mates wiggled free, and I tossed back just as many. None of them were truly right. Then one summer I had a bite on my line. It was my wife's heart. There was no way that I was tossing it back.

Financially, when I add it all up over the years, it cost me several hundred dollars of membership fees for the experiences—a small price to pay for such a unique perspective on dating. It cost my wife only a one-month membership fee to ChristianCafe.com. I have never seen someone receive such a big payoff for such a small investment of time and money.

Did I Provide for You What I Intended?

When I started writing this book, I wanted to share with you my experiences and what I learned. I believe that you will leave this experience more informed, a bit wiser, and more inspired. Here is a brief review of some of the key points:

- You should come away from this knowing that online dating can be a very effective way to find someone special.

- You should have hope not only because there are millions of people participating but also because my personal story is proof that it can work for you.

- You should understand that an investment of time and effort is necessary in order to have the happily-ever-after experience that you see on television.

- I left you with a few tricks that will help you derive the maximum benefit from this socializing tool (e.g., guidelines on when to meet someone, the two-by-four rule, the dynamics of international encounters).

- The communities of people looking for love online are vast and can be daunting. Consequently, it is important to maintain an attitude of moderation with the time that you invest.

So this has been my experience with online dating in a nutshell. It was honest. It was real. I will make the obvious even clearer by saying that I highly recommend that you consider using online dating to meet that special someone. If you have experience with online dating, it is time for a recommitment. If you are new to it or have been unsure, now is the time to make a positive change in your life.

Internet dating represents a fantastic new pathway that allows you to cross boundaries like never before. But then again, isn't that what the Internet is all about anyway—crossing boundaries, removing obstacles, integrating, and sharing? God has made so many wonderful people. Online dating is an easy way to meet some of them. Who knows? Your next true love could be waiting for you to post your profile and go fishing for love on the Net. Log on and see.

Endnotes

Chapter 1

1. Ellen Wernecke. "Joan Rivers Looks for Love on the Internet," March 10, 2006, http://www.thecelebritycafe.com/features/5211.html

2. U.S. Census Survey, September 2001, http://www.census.gov/population/socdemo/computer/ppl-175/tab01A.pdf

3. Staff Report, "Price of Love Rising as Online Dating Sites Boost Ads," Brandweek.com, February 27, 2007, http://www.brandweek.com/bw/news/recent_display.jsp?vnu_content_id=1003551150&imw=Y

4. Mayanna Dietz. "Online Dating Boom in Europe," CNN.com, February 15, 2002, http://archives.cnn.com/2002/TECH/Internet/02/13/Internet.dating/.

5. Neil Clark Warren, PhD. "Old Enough to Know," eHarmony.com, http://www.eharmony.com/singles/servlet/ncw/articles/rightage.

Chapter 2

1. Market Anomaly, "Soulless Radio Shack Fires 400 Employee by Email," September 21, 2006, http://www.marketanomaly.com/?p=212.

Chapter 3

1. http://www.divorcerate.org/.

2. Mabrey, Vicki. "Sexy Seniors Discover Pratfalls of Modern Love," Abcnews.com, November 30, 2006, http://abcnews.go.com/Nightline/story?id=2690251&page=1.

978-0-595-42491-7
0-595-42491-0

www.ingramcontent.com/pod-product-compliance
Lightning Source LLC
Chambersburg PA
CBHW051244050326
40689CB00007B/1056